The Quest for Peace

The Quest for Peace

A True Story of Courage and Faith In Life's Harshest Hours

Judith Glover

COVENANT
PUBLISHING

All Scripture questions, unless indicated, are taken from
THE INSPIRATIONAL BIBLE
Copyright © 1995, Word Publishing. All rights reserved.
"Scriptures quoted from The Holy Bible, New Century
Version, copyright © 1987, 1988, 1991 by Word Publishing,
Nashville, Tennessee. Used by permission."

International Standard Book Number 1-892435-09-8

To the honor, glory, and praise of
our Heavenly Father

Table of Contents

Acknowledgments

*F*rom the moment ideas for this book took root and grew, I made a promise to God that I would dedicate these words to him. Especially since I believed that God (along with much help and inspiration from the Holy Spirit) planted the seeds, watered, and nurtured their growth. Without his steadfast encouragement and guidance my discovery of inner peace would never have been realized. So, to the Godhead I offer my humble and deepest gratitude.

Many thanks to my dear, faithful, loving family that has given me so much encouragement: to David, my beloved husband, most valued critic and supporter; to Julie, my twin sister and her husband Najel; to Uncle John and Aunt Esther Bowman; to Uncle Wilfred Keene; to brothers and sisters-in-law Bob and Terry Glover, to Don and Barbara Glover, Bill and Joni Glover; to Bill and Joni's daughter Stephanie Glover, a lovely and very special young woman. Also, to my dear friends: to Ann Prichard Hanson, along with her daughter, Teri Stauffer, who played major roles in supporting and encouraging my efforts; to Laura Yee – what an inspiration you are to me – how I treasure your friendship; to Charlyn Kellar, along with her parents, Tom and Leah Tice, who "adopted" me and are such loving, godly servants; to Sue Meffan, and to Brenda and Marvin Williams, dear and deeply cherished friends; to Debra White Smith, Christie Craig,

Shirley Kervin, and Ronda Logan – friends who helped with proofing and typing the manuscript; to Edna Perry, a truly special friend and servant of the Lord; to Cherilyn Ziemer (Cherilyn's computer skills impressed me); to Sandra Backor and Tina Shoemaker, shining examples of encouragement and support to countless people – what wonderful friends you are; to Terry and Becki Cagle, amazing stewards of God's word; to Judy Miller and Tex Stevens for their glowing endorsements of this manuscript. Tex has been a dear friend to David and me for several years, and Judy is so precious! Through her diligent correspondence, God is blessing our blossoming friendship.

One of my greatest joys has been the renewing friendship with my college roommate, Charme Epperson Robarts. She, of all my friends, is at the top of my list of godly servants mirroring the image of Christ. She is one of God's lovely, "Charme"ing treasures.

Claire Ottenstein Ross, I cannot thank you enough. What a Godsend you have been. Your expertise and skill in editing and in critiquing this manuscript made it possible for me to take steps toward inner peace. What a beautiful and dear friend you are.

Lisa Sailor, a new friend and compelling witness for the Lord. You truly are unaware of your endearing testimony!

Edwin White, to whom I owe a special debt of thanks! For it was he who gave my manuscript to Steve Cable, and has worked with Steve in finalizing this book for publication.

To Steve Cable, my publisher. You will never truly know the depth of my gratitude; nor the number of prayers lifted to God in praise on your behalf. Continually I ask God to richly bless you and Covenant Publishing for seeing the potential of this work; and choosing to publish it. God is using you in countless ways to glorify His Name.

Again Steve, I cannot thank you enough!

Judith Moore Glover

Foreword

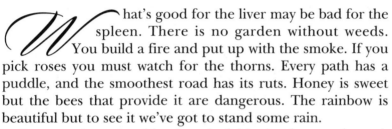hat's good for the liver may be bad for the spleen. There is no garden without weeds. You build a fire and put up with the smoke. If you pick roses you must watch for the thorns. Every path has a puddle, and the smoothest road has its ruts. Honey is sweet but the bees that provide it are dangerous. The rainbow is beautiful but to see it we've got to stand some rain.

It seems that everything wonderful is simultaneously terrible in some respect. Technology solves problems with new ones. Many computer users get painful carpal tunnel syndrome. Hospitals are good places to get an infection. Refrigeration makes summers more pleasant, but it's very expensive. The information age in which we live makes us all less private.

How are we to deal with life? Should we recoil in fear and despair just because things bite us back? Absolutely not! The Christ who died to save us lives to keep us. Christianity is not a way out but a way through. With God's help the difficulties of life make us better, not bitter. What the caterpillar calls the end of the world God calls a butterfly.

The message of this book is clear. Life is risky, but the Christian is always safe not in the absence of danger, but in the presence of God. The author argues that we find peace by enthroning Jesus in our hearts. We find peace in life, even with its hardships, if Christ strengthens us (Philippians 4:13).

With Christ, we love life even when we are sick and depressed. Christ enables us to find peace and get a kick out of life—even when life is a kick in the teeth. Faith makes it possible for us to see the nasty, painful things of life as a source of beauty, joy and strength. Faith understands that God often digs the wells of joy with the spade of sorrow. Every moment is golden for the one who has a vision of Christ.

Faith is important because, without it, a person thinks hard times, talks hard times, dreams hard times, and has hard times, most of the time. Christians are the happiest people alive. To the world they seem to have no particular reason for being happy and at peace with everything, but they are happy. They are happy because they know God has not left them alone. The songs in their hearts put smiles upon their faces. They know that God is good.

We are indebted to Judith Glover for telling her story. She is a survivor. It is always a wonderful thing to overcome problems, and the harder we fight, the more splendid the triumph. What we obtain cheaply, we appreciate little. Conquering any difficulty always gives us a secret joy. The words of this book reveal the joy of a woman who conquered by pushing on despite overwhelming obstacles. Her struggles resulted in growth.

My prayer is that God will give wings to Judith Glover's message. Everyone needs to read this book. No one is free of conflict and trouble. Life is no smooth road for anybody. Some are stimulated by the bracing atmosphere and roughness of life. Others, unfortunately, are destroyed. Strangely, the same circumstances overwhelm some while empowering others. What is the secret to empowerment? This book will help you to brace up, pray, trust, and find peace in life.

Edwin F. White
President, Covenant Publishing

Preface

he Bible often mentions inner peace. Surely these writers, especially the New Testament followers of Christ, and our Lord himself, would not have placed so much emphasis on inner peace if it were unattainable.

Mine is in no way an exhaustive study. These thoughts came to me during sleepless nights of pain brought on by multiple sclerosis. Through my 20-year struggle with this disease and my encounter along the way with a series of unexpected personal tragedies, I have been led into a deeper walk with God, which in turn has blessed me with greater discernment of the nature of inner peace and humanity's quest for it.

Popular songwriter and singer Amy Grant sings in one of her songs that the only good found in us is because of who God is. Surely we are responsible to open our lives to God in faith, longing for him to mold us into vessels fit for his service. For only in serving him can we find and maintain serenity in our souls. If we withhold our lives from God and hesitate to commit ourselves fully to achieving his purposes, he cannot bless us with his peace. When our faith in his power wavers, there remains only a belief system that relies on our own inadequate resources.

When we trust in our own power instead of his, inner peace is inconceivable to us. "God is able to do immeasurably more than we ask or imagine, because his power is at work within us," the Scriptures assure us (Ephesians 3:20). He empowers us with his Spirit, thus enabling peace to fill our souls. But this heaven-given serenity can be ours only when we acknowledge our total dependence on God and seek an abiding relationship with him.

To our shame, we often stifle and limit the working of God's Holy Spirit to help us achieve holiness, or peace, or any other characteristic of God. Jesus testifies that anything is possible for us, even if our faith is as small as a tiny mustard seed (Matthew 17:20). As incredible as it may seem to us in our moments of deep distress, the Lord can refresh even the most tumultuous heart with his peace. We open the door for his calming Presence when we allow the Holy Spirit to enable our belief that God can do all things in us and through us.

My prayer is that all who read this will be led into a deeper walk with God and will learn to trust him as the only true source of inner peace. The promise of Scripture is trustworthy and true to those who place their trust in the Lord: "God's peace, which is so great we cannot understand it, will keep your hearts and minds in Christ Jesus" (Philippians 4:7).

Chapter 1

The Beginning – My Journey Through Tears

"You have recorded my troubles. You have kept a list of my tears. Aren't they in your records?" (Psalm 56:8).

I was raised in a small midwestern town in Indiana. I grew up with my identical twin sister, Julie. Also, I had a brother, Jim (two years older), and a half-brother, Bob (seven years older). Our father cleared the land in the middle of acres of woods, then proudly and adeptly built our home along a creek surrounded by waterfalls and bluffs. It was a fairytale world filled with idyllic peace. Every day was a wonderland of imagination and adventure spent in exploring the woods, fishing, playing along soaring bluffs and in the cascading waterfalls. The trees often echoed our carefree laughter. I remember our futile attempts to catch the ever-elusive crawfish in their ceaseless scurry to submerged rocks in the creek. And, of course, in the winter there was always ice-skating and sledding. In this environment, I quickly learned to enjoy and appreciate the marvelously intriguing wonders of God's creation. During my times of reflection on those events and on my feeling so close to God in nature, I wrote the following poem:

God's Presence

Walking through the woods I see
Reflections of eternity
The Master's touch is everywhere
In mountain glen
And cougar's lair
Walking through the woods I see
Expressions of his majesty
His vivid strokes are clear to see
In meadow's green
And stately tree
Walking through the woods I see
Lessons in humility
In winter's grasp stillness lies
On frozen pond
As autumn dies
Walking through the woods I see
Images of heredity
To live with him we first must die
To self and sin
And Godless lives
Walking through his Word I see
Redeeming love and purity
Salvation flowed on splintered beam
In open tomb
Ascending scheme
Walking through his Word I see
Visions of serenity
With trumpet blast we're lifted high
To praise his Name
In Heavenly sky

As happy as I was in my childhood, I soon learned that life could also be terribly cruel and unmercifully vicious. Consequently, our Hoosier wonderland hallowed by my memories of its peacefulness became a refuge for me. There I learned to become a student of God's counsel. His sometimes-obscure Presence was revealed more tangibly because of his impressive, visible creation.

I don't remember exactly when my sexual "nightmare" began. Perhaps I've conveniently blocked it out. I believe it started when Julie and I were about five or six years old, perhaps earlier, and occurred often. A person our family highly respected and trusted sexually molested both of us. It was quite a shock. Whatever fondness we had for the man was lost, along with our innocence.

The abuse never happened while Julie and I were together, but we always suspected (perhaps because of our "twinness") that the other experienced it, too. Julie and I are extremely close, so it's ironic, but mostly sad that we never talked about these incidents until after I graduated from college. I think we would have developed a healthier self-respect and outlook on life if we had at least discussed it. Possibly, I was afraid to discover that if Julie was not molested, then I was singled out. If that were the case, I would feel responsible for the abuse.

In retrospect it's easy to see my lack of logic. But for a child whose capacity for logic hasn't fully developed, the conclusion that I was responsible for bringing the abuse on myself made perfect sense. Nevertheless, we did not confess the abuse to anyone until we were adults. As the years passed, it just seemed pointless to raise the issue with our parents. Whatever purpose confession served, it would result in terrible heartbreak for them. I just couldn't bring myself to afflict them with that burden and pain.

This is sad, too, because I always confessed everything to Mom. She told me that when I was little and was asked why we shouldn't do things that were wrong, I would reply, "Because it hurts God's heart!" In my childlike naiveté I reasoned, "God must not love me because I hurt him; so how could Mommy and Daddy love me either, if they knew what was happening to me? Especially since I must be responsible for it anyway."

These incidents left a horrid imprint on my life, with consequences reaching up through adolescence and extending into my adult years. The abuse had a definite bearing on the impressions I formed about myself and in the attitudes I developed regarding significant people in my life. From my distorted self-perception evolved insecurities, feelings of inadequacy, low self-esteem, and feelings of worthlessness. Mercifully, we had the proper nurturing and loving affection from our parents, and this went a long way in offsetting the negative touching we experienced from the molester. During these days God spoke to me in his words, "Do not let anyone treat you as if you are unimportant because you are young" (1 Timothy 4:12).

Through the years God has helped me come to terms with my feelings for the man who wronged me. He has led me to the point of forgiving him. Long ago he passed away. All I feel now is pity and sadness for him and for whatever circumstances provoked him to abuse us. I feel sadness for Julie and myself in that we lost our innocence and trust at such a painfully early age.

One reason I feel it necessary to address this heartbreaking issue is to stress the importance of forgetting the past. We must learn from the past, but we must let unpleasantness go. Wrongs done to us years ago must not dictate or justify our attitudes and behavior in the present. Inner peace is not attainable until we decide to put yesterday's' wounds behind us for good. I cannot change what happened then, but I am responsible for how I let it affect me now. In Max Lucado's God's Inspirational Promise Book, he writes:

> Bitterness is its own prison.
>
> The sides are slippery with resentment. A floor of muddy anger stills the feet. The stench of betrayal fills the air and stings the eyes. A cloud of self-pity blocks the view of the tiny exit above.
>
> Step in and look at the prisoners. Victims are chained to walls. Victims of betrayal. Victims of abuse.
>
> The dungeon, deep and dark, is beckoning you to enter . . . You can, you know. You've' experienced enough hurt . . .
>
> You can choose, like many, to chain yourself to your hurt . . .

18

Or you can choose, like some, to put away your hurts before they become hates . .

How does God deal with your bitter heart? He reminds you that what you have is more important than what you don't have. You still have your relationship with God. No one can take that.

All of his Christian life, the Apostle Paul was regretfully aware of how he had persecuted the Christians and thwarted the cause of Christ. And yet he said, "Forgetting the past and straining toward what is ahead, I keep trying to reach the goal and get the prize for which God has called me through Christ to life above" (Philippians 3:13-14).

Whether an individual is guilty of an unjust act or an innocent victim, forgiveness is a required step for any person who is seeking peace. We cannot have inner peace unless we recognize and practice God's commands to forgive and forget. Inner peace comes when we extend forgiveness and forget the bitterness. The story of Paul's conversion (Acts 9:1-19) is a striking testimony:

> So he went to the high priest and asked him to write letters to the synagogues in the city of Damascus. Then if Saul found any followers of Christ's' Way, men or women, he would arrest them . . . So Saul headed toward Damascus. As he came near the city, a bright light from heaven suddenly flashed around him. Saul fell to the ground and heard a voice saying to him, "Saul, Saul! Why are you persecuting me?" Saul said, "Who are you Lord?" The voice answered, "I am Jesus, whom you are persecuting." . . . The Lord said to Ananias, "Go! I have chosen Saul for an important work. He must tell about me to those who are not Jews, to kings, and to the people of Israel. I will show him how much he must suffer for my name." So Ananias went to the house of Judas. He laid his hands on Saul and said, "Brother Saul, the Lord Jesus sent me. He is the one you saw on the road on your way here. He sent me so that you can see again and be filled with the Holy Spirit." Then Saul got up and was baptized.

19

When Paul was convicted in his heart that he had sinned, he immediately repented and received forgiveness from God. This forgiveness was received when his sins were washed away with Jesus' blood. His faith led him to baptism (Acts 22:16). God also sent his servant, Ananias, to instruct Paul in the Scriptures. Consequently, Paul forgave himself and put his misdeeds behind him. From that point on, Paul enjoyed peace in Christ, which manifested itself in devout service and dedication to the cause of Christ. Paul had a heavy load of guilt to bear and a great deal of forgetting to master. To his credit, and through God's enlightenment, Paul could put these things behind him and divert his energies into zealous work for the Lord.

In the Old Testament, Joseph is another example of forgiveness. The account of Joseph occurs in Chapters 37-50 of Genesis. His brothers are insanely jealous because he is their father's' favorite son. Consequently, they plot to kill him, but decide instead to go with the lesser evil of selling him into slavery. They further compound the misdeed by telling their aging father that an animal killed Joseph.

Joseph eventually becomes a slave to Potiphar, one of Pharaoh's officials. Because God is with Joseph, he prospers there. Unfortunately, Potiphar's wife falsely accuses Joseph of making advances toward her, a charge that costs him several years of imprisonment. Even in this, God is with him so that he receives favorable treatment.

Eventually officials summon Joseph to Pharaoh's palace to interpret the king's dreams. When he correctly interprets these dreams, Pharaoh makes him second in command and ruler over the land of Egypt.

Famine ravages the land and Jacob, Joseph's father, sends Joseph's brothers to Egypt to buy grain. Here they unknowingly transact their business with Joseph, who immediately recognizes them. Joseph has plenty of reasons for holding grudges against these men, but he gladly forgives them. When he meets his brothers for the first time, you can still feel his vulnerability and pain, though he has come to realize that what they had intended for evil, God meant for good.

"Then Joseph said to them, 'Don't be afraid. Can I do what only God can do? You meant to hurt me, but God turned your evil into good to save the lives of many people, which is being done. So don't' be afraid. I will take care of you and your children.' So he comforted his brothers and spoke kind words to them" (Genesis 50:19-21). God's power enables us, like Joseph, to forgive and forget major offenses against us, and even to go the extra mile.

I link my story of abuse in a very personal way to Joseph's story of suffering and subsequent forgiveness of his abusers. Unquestionably, something dreadful happened to Julie and me. I lived under its cloud until God opened my eyes to the damage I inflicted on myself by not forgetting and forgiving. Today I know the wisdom and truth of Jesus' words, "If you forgive others their sins, your Father in heaven will also forgive you for your sins. But if you don't' forgive others, your Father in heaven will not forgive your sins" (Matthew 6:14-15).

Inner peace is impossible while we embrace malice toward someone else. The writer of Colossians admonishes us to "get along with each other, and forgive each other. If someone does wrong to you, forgive that person because the Lord forgave you . . . Let the peace that Christ gives control your thinking, because you were all called together in one body to have peace" (Colossians 3:13-15).

Chapter 2

Growing Through Grief and Tragedy

"With all the violence and murder and killings we've had in the United States, I think you will agree that we must keep firearms from people who have no business with guns."

– Robert F. Kennedy (May 1968, five days before his assassination)

God created us and knows our fragile natures. He mercifully prevents us from having foreknowledge of events that reduce our secure worlds to over whelming sorrow. I say this to preface my account of the tragedy that obliterated our family's piously naïve illusion. We thought ourselves exempt from the criminal savagery people read about in the headlines every day. "That just happens on TV and in the movies, not to good, decent people like us. After all, we're Christians! Yes, I know we're not always faithful, but God overlooks that, doesn't he? Surely he owes us exemption from suffering and trials because we went under the water of baptism for him. Surely he doesn't expect any more from us than that."

How God must grieve at our flippant penchant for minimizing our service and praise to him. We expect him to step in and disrupt the laws of nature simply because we wear his name. I don't mean to imply that we should not pray for him to intervene when tragedies happen. I've wished often that God had reached down and jammed the trigger or bent the firing pin or somehow stopped the shotgun blast that ripped my brother's head from his body.

April 26, 1970, had been a particularly exhausting day. Our high school was the host to the State Track and Field competitions. Julie and I helped in various capacities. That evening we attended a banquet and dance, celebrating the end of the school year. It was a long, tiring day, so I was ready to tumble into bed for a refreshing night's sleep.

Around 11:30 p.m., however, I was awakened with an uneasy feeling that I couldn't quite put my finger on. A nagging premonition that something was wrong troubled me. I remember thinking that Jim, then 18, was out after curfew, which was uncharacteristic for him. But that was his problem, not mine. I turned over and went back to sleep.

A few hours later I was again aroused from slumber by a persistent knocking on the door. We lived out of town and didn't lock our doors at night. So I knew it wasn't Jim wanting in. Since my bedroom was nearest the door, I got up and opened it to find two police officers standing there. Immediately I knew something must be wrong with Jim. They asked me to get my dad. Dad told me to go back to bed and then went outside to talk with them on the porch. I could hear Daddy coughing nervously, but I couldn't make out the conversation. Eventually, the police left. Dad then came into our room and sat on the bed. From his expression, Julie and I knew something dreadful had happened. Finally, with a heavy sigh, he said, "Girls, Jim's been killed! Jimmy's dead!"

Julie immediately began sobbing, but for some reason, I couldn't get out a single tear. I remember wondering what was wrong with me that I could not show any emotion. We were extremely close. Why wasn't I crying? My teeth began to chatter and my body began to shake uncontrollably. I felt as though my emotions were caught and held defenseless. It was as if I had been exposed to an arctic blast of subfreezing temperature that had swept in and taken control of my body. I was cold – painfully cold.

All of us were in a state of shock. Mom was a registered nurse. Since she was working the late shift in a hospital 25 miles away, she hadn't been told yet. Dad called her sister who lived in the city where Mom worked, and Mom's brother-in-law brought her home, only telling her that Jim had been shot and killed. I will never ever forget the emotions that played across her face when Dad gave her the details. Her shock, disbelief, and horror, mirrored in our faces as well. Mom's face just seemed to crumple and age right there before our eyes.

Let me regress here for a moment to Jim's infancy. He was born prematurely (at six and a half months), weighing just three pounds. He lived in an incubator for several weeks. Finally the doctor, knowing Mom was an R.N., allowed her to take Jim home with instructions to feed him every two hours for two months.

At eleven months, he went back to the hospital with suspected meningitis or polio. They placed him in the isolation ward with the restriction of "No Visitors!" They later discovered that he had pneumonia, but kept him in isolation because there were no available beds in pediatrics.

Mom and Dad tried desperately to persuade the staff to let them go in to be with him. Since there were no other patients in the ward, it was really ridiculous and heartless that they were bound to rules that no longer applied. Nevertheless, they could not enter and were limited to just waving at little Jimmy through the window. And, of course, he would wave back and cry to be with them.

Daddy finally got so disgusted and frustrated that he marched into the ward, past the protesting nurses, picked Jimmy up, and took him home without a doctor's release. Fortunately, there were no repercussions. It's anyone's guess how long Jim would have remained in the hospital if Dad hadn't taken some action. Jim was walking at the time he was admitted to the hospital, but by the time he came home he had rubbed his little knees raw from crawling around his crib in the hospital. What I'm saying is that Mom and Dad had a tremendous investment of time and energy in Jim's survival. So to lose him in such a horrible manner, in the prime of his life, was a devastating blow to them.

We received the story of Jim's death from his best friend, Greg, who was with him at the time and witnessed the tragic event (all names are changed, except Jim's). They had stopped by Howie's apartment (another friend) to pick up Howie's cousin, John, to go to Mr. Donut in a nearby town. After waiting an hour or so, Jim told them that if they were not going anywhere, then he ought to go on home since he was going to help his dad paint the house the next morning. Howie informed all of them plainly that no one was going anywhere! Going to his closet, supposedly to get his jacket, he emerged instead with a shotgun, and began laughing and kidding around. Impersonating James Cagney, he pointed the gun at each of them. When he came to Jim, he pointed it at his face and pulled the trigger at point blank range. Greg told us later that he feared for all of their lives and was going to testify against Howie in court.

I try not to visualize what it must have been like for Dad to identify Jim's body. He seemed to age ten years from the ordeal. Understandably, Jim's coffin was closed. I used to fantasize that he wasn't really dead, that the casket was empty and he was involved in some top-secret government project that required him to go into hiding for the rest of his life. Somehow, that seemed easier to deal with than the reality that he had been taken from us in such a horribly brutal way. Of course, I have eventually faced reality and accepted the fact that we would no longer have Jim with us.

The trial proceedings were a real fiasco. Our town was in the process of electing new county officials, so the prosecuting attorney changed in midstream. Before this happened, though, Mom and Dad confided in an attorney who led them to believe that he would take their case. According to Mom, they learned later that the same lawyer had already agreed to defend Howie. They were astonished.

Newspaper accounts implied that a big party was going on at the time of Jim's death. Howie had been drinking, but the autopsy report verified that there was no substance abuse of any kind found in Jim's body. Jim and Greg had arrived on the party scene after everyone but John had left.

Jim lettered in varsity football for three years and could run the 100-yard dash in 9.6. He had a quiet, shy nature, but he also loved to tease and wasn't afraid to enjoy himself. Consequently, he never lacked friends. He enjoyed nature immensely and hoped to be a forest ranger someday. I admit that I'm biased, but very few who knew him would disagree with my description of his character. He was a special young man, a quality person.

The grand jury gathered enough evidence to show that his death was not an accident, so they bound Howie over for trial. The trial date was nearly a year after the incident occurred. By this time, Howie's parents had hired a prestigious lawyer. According to Mom, the new prosecuting attorney did not even look at our case or the coroner's report before the trial. He seemed to care little about the outcome. Mom and Dad were so frustrated that they hired a lawyer from another town. At least this attorney saw the seriousness of the case, and we finally had some hope that justice would prevail.

When the trial day finally arrived, we were dutifully there at 8:00 a.m. With reluctance and heavy hearts, we entered the courtroom. We were relieved that the legal process was moving now, and we were urgent to get it done and to put this day behind us so that we could go on with our lives as best we could. However, we were about to have another rude awakening to the callousness of this world's "justice."

When lunchtime rolled around, the trial adjourned. The judge, lawyers, and Howie still deliberated behind closed doors. They had not yet made an appearance. After lunch they again cloistered themselves behind closed doors for another hour. When at last they emerged, our sighs of relief soon caught in our throats. They informed us that Howie plea-bargained and would be found guilty only of involuntary manslaughter. He received ten-years probation, of which he served only six months.

We were stunned. How could that be possible when there was so much evidence showing otherwise? At least they should have let Greg testify against him. We wanted to hear and see something to show that the law is for the rights of the victim.

27

I cried, "God, where are you? How can you let this happen? Why do you let us continue to suffer like this? Don't you see the injustice of it all? Why don't you do something? It isn't right! It just isn't fair!"

As I look back on those events, I realize that I felt like Jonah when he cried out to God, "So now I ask you, Lord, please kill me. It is better for me to die than to live." Then the Lord said, "Do you think it is right for you to be angry" (Jonah 4:3-4)?

One of the daily passages in the Women's Devotional Bible Calendar says:

> *Life isn't always the way we want it to be;*
> *it doesn't always seem fair, in our eyes or from our*
> *perspective, that is. But all is fair and just in God's eyes.*
> *And we must resist the urge to doubt or judge like Jonah.*
>
> *– Doris Rikkers*

They say time heals all wounds, but the scars remain forever. What we learn from those scars is up to us. Our relationship with God has a definite bearing on our state of mind when tragedies occur. Whether we fall apart and become bitter, or bear up to trials with God's sustaining peace, is up to us. Jesus said, "You can have peace in me. In this world you will have trouble, but be brave! I have defeated the world" (John 16:33). When engulfed in all this anguish over Jim's death, we were not faithful Christians, and this tragedy pushed us even farther from God. Fortunately, we later returned to the church and to God, who enabled us to resolve our conflicts and come to a place of peace and forgiveness toward Howie.

Here again I stress the fundamental importance that forgiveness plays in the heart of any individual truly seeking peace. Without compassion and humility on our part, we will never find peace and rest. How can we possibly justify wearing Christ's name if we are not willing to forgive, since this is the essence of God? I confess that I would like to have seen Howie serve some form of sentence or incarceration for taking my brother's life. But whether he is literally behind bars or not, I can't help but believe that he is serving time behind the bars of his mind. He is confined and caged with his thoughts and the gory scenes of shedding innocent blood for the rest of his life. I do feel sorry for anyone who must live with such memories.

God makes no guarantees that our suffering and trials will cease once we put on his name, but he does offer us peace through his Son. "I leave peace, my peace I give you. I do not give it to you as the world does. So don't let your hearts be troubled or afraid" (John 14:27). I know that when we're in the midst of suffering and anguish, peace seems like such an obscure hope. God enables us to realize its reality when our minds recognize and accept his supreme knowledge and wisdom in all matters that pertain to us. We will always have questions with no answers. "There are some things the Lord our God has kept secret" (Deuteronomy 29:29). But peace is developed in a sincere, abiding relationship with God that transcends all understanding. Peace comes despite the circumstances and trials that plague our existence in a sinful, evil world.

Mom wrote the following poem after Jim's death. Her example of strength and trust in God comforted me. Clearly, she was a student of God's counsel and walked the roads of inner peace with him.

Fearless Hearts

Our path ahead looked bright and cheerful
Without a cloud to dim our way
We had no need for being fearful
And lived with joy from day to day

Then, suddenly, a dark cloud hovered
Our way grew dark and soon joy fled
We found all our signposts covered
And strained to see our way ahead

But, we trusted God to lead us
Down the path he would have us go
For we knew that he would guide us
Though his plan we did not know

So with fearless hearts we follow
All the turns our new path brings
For now we know the fearful darkness
Was just the shadow of his wings

—Roberta Moore, 1970

All of us will have darkness in our lives. We have nothing to fear if we know that adversity is just the shadow of his wings. What a beautiful, consoling thought!

The Acceptance of Suffering

*"When I suffer, this comforts me: Your promise
gives me life" (Psalm 119:50).*

s mentioned previously, I have multiple sclerosis. It is a disease of the central nervous system. Its
cause and cure remain unknown. Our nerves have
protective sheaths around them and MS is a breakdown of
this protective covering due to plaque in the brain and spinal
column. Consequently, messages from the brain are either
blocked or delayed. Thus, a message may get distorted (so
that cold water feels extremely hot). A message may not be
received at all (so that the bladder refuses to empty).
Symptoms include unsteady gait, loss of balance, and slurred
speech. This can be amusing to an unsuspecting observer.
More than once I've received a raised eyebrow from those
who don't know my problem. Sometimes a creeping numb-
ness spreads throughout the body, or it confines itself to one
or more extremities. Other symptoms include spastic move-
ments, progressive weakness, paralysis, extreme fatigue,
visual difficulties, and bladder dysfunction, which frequently
lead to urinary tract infections.

Sometimes I experience very strange sensations in the
affected areas, such as deep, intense burning where nerves
feel like they are laid bare and exposed to direct, searing
heat. At other times, tingling makes me feel like all the bones

in my body are literally going crazy, and I frequently feel a vice like pressure around my chest. Intellectual functioning may also be hindered at times. My memory may be affected. I may find myself unable to solve problems that require extended concentration and organization. When that happens, I jokingly say that I've become a "no brainer." (Hey! you've got to have a sense of humor.) Generally, because of my MS, I am in constant pain (sometimes to the point of nausea). However, my pain is rarely obvious to the casual observer.

As you can imagine, all of this has taught me a valuable lesson about our inclination to judge one another. When we take it upon ourselves to judge others, we invariably base our decisions on outward appearances only. Thus, we may assess the person's physical needs but fail to consider his inner struggles. Often, if our internal needs are provided, then the physical needs are much easier to endure.

Sometimes the person in need may rebuff or dismiss the truly sincere individual who wishes to help. This rejection may be due to a consideration for the individual's time. Or it may happen simply because the situation is so overwhelming that the sufferer doesn't feel comfortable unloading huge problems onto others. Experience has taught me, however, that in rebuffing offers of aid we often keep God from working through them to help us. They are unable to share our burdens and give us the comfort and support we need.

I find myself limiting God in this area. I may look fine when inwardly I am experiencing many forms of suffering. It just seems heartless to explain how I'm really feeling because there is nothing anyone can do. So I just smile and evade the issue, usually by changing the subject. It is often hard for me to accept offers of help. But I'm learning to be more discerning of other's responses to the question, "How are you doing?" I know that there are countless people who suffer on the inside while they smile on the outside. In all honesty, I learned this lesson years ago, but I am reminded of it more frequently now because of my present pain. Hopefully this has made me more patient with myself and with others, less judgmental of other's actions, and more receptive of God's ministering through caring family and friends. Patiently and tenderly, God reinforces my inner peace daily by these kind acts of love and support. The psalmist was right when he wrote, "Examine and see how good the Lord is. Happy is the person who trusts him" (Psalm 34:8).

When physical relapses occur, the most difficult symptoms for me to deal with are the sciatic nerve pain and extreme fatigue. Even if I've slept 10 to12 hours, just taking a shower and preparing to go somewhere can drain me of all energy. Consequently, I've learned to pace myself and to allow plenty of time to complete ordinary tasks. I allow longer time for the more difficult ones. Reluctantly, I've learned to limit my activities.

Because I realize the importance of being with positive, happy people, sometimes it seems like I'm in an endless battle with Satan over mind control. If I'm not careful, I find myself being the only guest at my own pity-party. Fortunately God rescues me, but not without some effort on my part. I find that reading the Bible or other books on encouragement and motivation gives me excellent tools for positive thinking. So do the acts of praying or reaching out to someone in need. Also, I enjoy nature tremendously. So when I am able, I never turn down opportunities to go walking in the woods or to sit outside under the trees. It seems to rejuvenate my outlook on life, refresh my faith in God, and bring peace to my soul.

Helen Keller, who overcame great disabilities in her life, said, "Character cannot be developed in ease and quiet. Only through experiences of trial and suffering can the soul be strengthened, vision cleared, ambition inspired, and success achieved."

While reading the book, *Disappointment With God* by Philip Yancey, I noticed with interest that he addressed the "unfairness of life" issue. The following insightful comments come from a man he calls Douglas: "If we develop a relationship with God apart from life circumstances . . . then we probably will be able to hang on when the physical reality breaks down. We can learn to trust God despite all the unfairness of life. Isn't that really the main point of Job?" Yancey then concludes: "It occurred to me as I read the Gospels that if all in his Body would spend our lives as he did – ministering to the sick, feeding the hungry, resisting the powers of evil, comforting those who mourn, and bringing the Good News of love and forgiveness – then perhaps the question, 'Is God unfair?' would not be asked with such urgency today."

Douglas' story made such an impact on me because his sentiments reflected mine. I can honestly say that I have never blamed God for my adversities. To do so would be putting myself above even God himself. What arrogance I would have! No. My response to this has always been, "Why should I be spared from suffering? It is part of life. Jesus was not even spared and he was perfect."

Frankly, MS can be a highly frustrating disease, and a scary one at times. Relapses come without warning, and I never know how many areas it will affect, to what degree, or how long the symptoms will last. Fortunately, I do eventually go into partial remission, usually after three or four months.

Since the initial onslaught in December of 1981, I have been hospitalized repeatedly, generally for testing, dehydration, or for intravenous steroid treatments. Once, however, I went to the Emergency Room because of an acute, adverse reaction to ACTH, a cortisone drug. I received daily injections of this drug on a trial basis. By the sixth day I was at my maximum dosage. That evening I began to feel extremely weak and lethargic. It was an effort just to breathe, and I experienced an excruciating headache. Fortunately I was with my retired-nurse mother, and for some reason I asked her to take my blood pressure. It was 220/110. She immediately took me to the hospital, and then the real adventure began.

Mercifully, I have a high tolerance for pain, but that was an experience I never want to repeat. The doctors and nurses were shamefully overworked, understaffed, and trying desperately to find places for the sudden onslaught of patients. They were forced to place some of us on beds in the hallways. Finally, after two hours, they put me into a room with a man. By that time, my vanity and embarrassment were thrown to the wind. I was vomiting from the pain and literally could not lie still because of it. The staff couldn't reach my doctor and could not give me anything for pain until they heard from him. Four hours later, after x-rays and a visit from the doctor on call, they finally gave me Demerol. I was told to quit ACTH cold turkey, but I was to confirm this with my doctor the following morning. They did not have to twist my arm to get me to agree with them on that decision. It was quite a humbling experience, especially the discovery that I wasn't so invincible to pain as I thought I was. From that experience I gained a finer appreciation for the frailty of life and the value of each day God allows me.

My next stay in the hospital reinforced this insight. From time to time I mentioned it to different doctors, but I always got the response that pain was a symptom of MS and that I would have to learn to live with it. Thankfully, my neurologist suggested that I have an MRI (Magnetic Resonance Imaging) scan of my spine. From this study my doctors discovered that I had a herniated disc. They scheduled me for surgery within a week. The surgery went well and in a matter of three days I was discharged from the hospital. By mid-afternoon, however, I ran a low-grade fever. Symptoms grew more severe through the night and into the morning. When Mom talked with my surgeon, he told her I would be readmitted to the hospital that morning. That was the last thing I wanted to hear, but by that evening I was glad to be there. My temperature spiked to 105 degrees.

I have often wondered if the nurse that night was a visiting angel. In the ten days I was there I never saw her again, but I believe she saved my life that night. The following story, *Angel With A Red Hat*, by Tami Fox, reminds me that sometimes we really might entertain angels:

I was so scared but would not admit it, as I sat in the coffee shop across from the Mayo Clinic. Tomorrow I would be a patient there, undergoing spinal surgery. The risk was high, but

35

my faith was strong. Just weeks before, I sat through my father's funeral. "O heavenly Father, in my time of trial, send me an angel."

As I looked up, preparing to leave, I saw an elderly lady walking very slowly to the register. I stood behind her, admiring her flair for fashion – a bright paisley dress of red and purple, a scarf, a brooch, and a brilliant scarlet hat. "Excuse me, madam. I just must say what a beautiful woman you are. You've made my day."

She clasped my hand and spoke these words: "My sweet child, bless you, for you see, I have an artificial arm and a plate in the other, and my leg is not my own. It takes me much time to get dressed. I try to do my best, but as the years go by, people don't seem to think it matters. You've made me feel so special today. May the Lord watch over you and bless you, for you must be one of his little angels." When she walked away from me that day, I uttered not a word, for she had touched my soul so that only she could have been the angel.

The Scripture tells us, "Remember to welcome strangers, because some who have done this have welcomed angels without knowing it" (Hebrews 13:2).

My nurse (angel?) had an assistant, and between the two of them they earned their pay and more. Constantly they checked my vital signs, and they kept me packed in ice and sponged down with cold towels. The worst part was when they put me on a hypothermia blanket. It was so cold it hurt, and my leg muscles began to go into spasms. I have to admit I cried. It was unbearable. All I wanted was to get rid of that thing, but the nurses and my mom held me down, practically in tears themselves. Mercifully, my temperature began to edge down so that I might find release from that torture.

Attending nurses and my doctor explained that before my back surgery I received an antibiotic to clean my intestines of all bacteria. Evidently, one toxic strain remained. Since there was nothing left in my intestines to feed on, the bacteria began eating on my intestinal walls. I endured endless tests until finally this one came back positive. By this time I had gone nearly a week with only ice chips to chew on or juice to sip. Moreover, I had not lost my appetite so I was very hungry. I was actually excited when they let me eat some Jell-O. After release from the hospital, my surgeon told me that this toxic strain of bacteria was potentially lethal.

One thing I've discovered through all of this is that I can deal with my relapses more easily than my family and friends can. I believe it is because God has taught me that we can only live one day at a time. Do the best you can with today. God doesn't expect more from us. He does not even assure us of another day.

Paradoxically, I can accept the suffering in my own life, but I don't want to accept the suffering in other's lives. Although I realize that suffering, if endured with much faith and prayer, can bring glory to God, I don't want those people close to me to experience pain. Obviously this is a ridiculous notion. No matter how desperately we try to protect and shield our loved ones from suffering, it is inevitable since Satan is roaming the earth (1 Peter 5:8). All we can do is prayerfully seek peace with God and trust him to see us through. If we are looking to him, he will see to our encouragement and support always.

To help illustrate this point, my dear friend, Laura Yee, has agreed to let me share the story of her daughter's battle with a cancerous brain tumor. The following is an excerpt from our conversation. I find her story profoundly moving as she touches on their pain and struggle. She reveals their victory with God in Jodi's miraculous recovery:

Jodi's ordeal began in 1986. Then she was only three years old. When I first found out that Jodi had a tumor, I really had great faith that we would have the surgery and she would be okay. I felt grateful that strong, faithful Christians were at the hospital with us during the surgery. The people that came were encouraging and I felt that God would listen to their prayers.

When one of her surgeons said, "Don't expect her to live but a couple of years," I still had much faith. You don't face it until it's just thrown in your face. You never even think about it. I guess you do in the back of your mind, but you think this could never happen to me.

Henry, my husband, was really struggling then. Our prayer life became very strong. Henry still prayed and believed God could do what he wanted to do, but he had never seen it happen in an almost miraculous way. He had seen little things, but never saw something big that would cause him to say, "Wow! That is definitely God!"

When it [the tumor] grew back, I got quite angry. Except that we were told by another surgeon, "it's a different kind of tumor than what we thought. If I get it all it won't grow back." So I thought God was just guiding us to this doctor. He was the answer to our prayers. "See, I told you, Henry! That's the way it works." At that point my concerns ceased and I thought it would never grow back. But when it did return, my faith really dropped. The doctor said the tumor wasn't what he thought it was. It was the kind that would always grow back. There was nothing to stop it, but they would try radiation. We sent Jodi's records to Houston specialists, who confirmed that there was a 10-25% chance that she would live to five years of age.

I was furious. Then I was reading the book, Why Bad Things Happen to Good People, written by a Jewish rabbi who believed that God had the power to change things but didn't intervene. His son died at age twelve from the aging disease. The rabbi became bitter. Instead of realizing there was a reason for that to happen, he thought of it as a cruel joke. Therefore, he reasoned, God could not do such a horrid thing, and the rabbi was in jeopardy of losing his faith.

I would read that and think, "Why? Why? What did Jodi do?" There is no good that could ever come from this. Nothing good would ever come from my daughter suffering. Maybe death could serve some good purpose, but not suffering. I didn't understand why he would let little children suffer. The rabbi believed that a loving and just God could not do this.

I realized that God couldn't be understood or described in human terms. The elders came over to pray with us. They said, "we're doing this for you, but also, we're doing this for us. Prayer makes us stronger. It makes our faith stronger as well as yours." Jodi may die. I've got to look at it that way, too! But, I've got to believe there is a reason. God never promises anywhere that we will not suffer. I think that is a misconception of Christians. We think that if we believe and if we have a strong faith, then nothing "bad" will happen to us. But the hard things are what make us strong. Those are the things that are going to help us get to Heaven. That's God's concern. He cares about our physical health, but it's nothing compared to the health of our soul.

I did go through a really long, hard time. It was difficult going to church. I was so angry! I don't know what brought me through that trial. I think it was people praying for me because they saw what I was going through, and they saw the doubt I had.

Now, when I question God's decisions, I go to Romans 11:33: "Yes, God's riches are very great, and his wisdom and knowledge have no end! No one can explain the things God decides or understand his ways . . . Who has known the mind of the Lord, or who has been able to give him advice?" And, "Yes, God made all things, and everything continues through him and for him. To him be the glory forever! Amen." It must be to the glory of God no matter what – good and bad. He never promised that I would have good health or that my children would have good health and that nothing bad would happen to us. But he did promise me that I would get through it and I could be stronger as a result. I've got to remember that promise because I can't do it on my own.

I used to pray all day long, "You've got to heal her. Please heal her." It drove me crazy. I couldn't get it off my mind. I thought that the more I prayed to God, the more likely it would be that he would change his mind. Finally I started praying, "Just give me strength to get through whatever is going to happen and help me to be the kind of mother Jodi

39

needs." When I changed my attitude about it, I found peace. I wasn't fighting with him anymore. You can't fight with God. I do ask for Jodi's healing, but I say, "Whatever your plan, I won't stop loving you, and I won't stop having faith in you. You will still be my God. Just help me get through it." That's when I found peace.

Another way I changed my attitude was to thank God for today and for the year. It's been more than a year since the radiation. They told us that radiation would give her only six months and then it would start growing back. So, I thank him for today. Jodi's prayers are so precious. It's been such awful weather here—115 degrees. She says, "Thank you, God, for this wonderful day." To her, it was! She doesn't pray that God will heal her. She believes healing took place already. She says, "Thank you for making me better," and prays for her friends. Her prayers are just so sweet. Jodi's life is such a glory to God, especially since the doctors only gave her a 10% chance of survival. I don't think they even believed that. They just wanted to give us something. But right now, today, Jodi's life is a glory to God. And if she dies, then there is a reason for it, and glory will come from it. I've wished a million times that I, not Jodi, was afflicted. "Just give it to me!" Satan chose a child to upset us all. He wanted our faith weak. Instead, God gave us greater strength to handle the outcome.

Laura's words ministered to me in my own struggle. They made me think of an insight by Hannah Whithall Smith:

Even to ourselves come afflictions that we cannot understand, and Satan seems so busy in the matter that it is hard to trace the hand of the Lord in it at all. But his hand is in it nevertheless, and he over- rules everything. No trial comes except by his permission and for some wise and loving purpose, which perhaps only eternity will disclose.

This is a poem I wrote after watching the despair of Laura and her family. It helped me to deal with Jodi's suffering.

Despair

Helpless! We watch the path of disease,
As it randomly strikes its pleasure to seize.

"Why one so young?" We ask in despair.
"It doesn't seem right! It just isn't fair!"

With grief and frustration we do what we can,
But silently knowing it's out of our hands.

Baffled and weary with tortured unrest,
Our prayers go unanswered and lengthen the stress.

Heavy the burden we quietly bear,
Too heavy to carry, or even to share.

Believing you loved us, unfailing in care,
With wavering faith we doubt you are there.

For what loving Father would allow us such grief,
And turn from our pleading to bring us relief?

No words of comfort or scripture of gain,
Will lessen this anguish or ease us of pain.

Hopeless and weary we struggle each day.
Abandoned! You left us to go on your way!

Just lead us and guide us in all we can ask–
We no longer know our measure of task.

Perhaps you'll reveal it, for now it's unclear.
We battle against it with heartache and fear.

Jodi's tired little body bravely succumbed to the relentless and savage assault of pain from her tumors. She died April 2, 1993, at the age of ten. These comforting words are from the Women's Devotional Bible Calendar:

> *"The Lord gives us others who are like velvet, whose words are comforting and supportive. They are the soft cushions we need when we are scraped with the 'sandpapers' and can listen to us as we explore the weaknesses and needs they bring out in us. They tangibly reveal God's perspective – just when we need it"* *(Kathy Narramore and Alice Hill).*

Shortly after Jodi's death, Laura discovered that she also had a rare form of leukemia. More recently, she discovered an abdominal tumor that required a hysterectomy. She tries to deal valiantly with these traumatizing hardships. Laura is a faithful, loving friend. I treasure her friendship beyond life itself. I would willingly take on her disease. She has suffered so much hardship and pain. How true is Carol Kuykendall's precious thought: "As a friend, I can't heal or change a painful situation. But I can listen . . . with ears that open into my heart."

Laura's' friendship means much to me. When I met her after my move to Arizona in 1977, she took me to meet all of her family. From that point on they took me in as part of their family. We celebrated every holiday and birthday, took several trips together to California to visit relatives, and went to Disneyland. There were many other trips to the mountains of Arizona and countless domino and card games – all shared with her family. They adopted us. And what a marvelous, loving family they have proved to be. Even after I moved to Texas, I've been extremely fortunate to get to return to Arizona several times a year. The ties that bind us are such sweet blessings from God.

Laura and I once talked about death. With tears in her eyes, she said that she wanted to make a very special request of me. I agreed without asking any questions, although I was curious. She was obviously troubled about something. She asked, "We don't know if there will be mothers in Heaven, but if there are, would you be Jodi's mother if you get to Heaven before I get there?" I was deeply moved by her request because it showed how much she thought of me.

Laura misses Jodi so much. She goes to the cemetery often. Once a month she takes a gallon of water, a dry towel, scissors, and artificial flowers to groom and freshen Jodi's grave marker. She washes and dries it with the towel and then arranges the new flowers around it. It is also touching to see her go to other grave markers and clean them as well. But as she tended to Jodi's, I could almost feel her pain, and I could definitely see her tender, loving care. So for Laura to make that request of me was a tremendous honor and one that I will cherish until I die—and beyond.

I learned from Jodi's suffering (and mine) to trust God's judgment, and I tried to encourage Laura in her ordeal. During this I also learned the value of writing my thoughts down. Surprisingly to me, writing journals proved therapeutic and it enhanced my prayer life, which in turn, allowed me to find deeper peace.

The following is a paraphrase I wrote of Proverbs 3:5-6, one of my favorite passages from the Bible about trusting in God:

Up Close and Personal

I trust in the Lord with all my heart, soul and mind
Depending not on my faulty human understanding.
In everything I do I will strive to know God more completely;
ever seeking to give God the glory and praise.
When I pursue this attitude of reverence and respect for God,
he continues to direct my life down straight paths of peace that
lead to his eternal home.

Laura asked me how I felt about my own suffering. I replied that I surely don't enjoy it, but I will never blame God for it. Why would I feel I should be exempt from suffering? I agree with Laura. God never promised that we would live on Easy Street once we became his children. Jesus wasn't spared. Why should I be? Moreover, this idea of guaranteed health is a gross misrepresentation of Christianity. If we teach it, then we set people up for a fall. To teach guaranteed health and happiness is a travesty of God's word. People duped into believing such assurances, and who then encounter crushing tragedies, often leave the church thinking they were better off in the world. "It would have been better for them to have never known the right way than to know it and to turn away from the holy teaching that was given to them" (2 Peter 2:21).

I don't mean to paint a bleak picture of Christianity or to belabor the issue of suffering. But because Satan introduced sin into the world, suffering is definitely a part of this life, whether we follow Christ or not. However, there is one comforting, fundamental difference. It is the fact that Christians have God's love and care revealed and expressed to them tangibly through the encouragement and support we share with one another.

The apostles Peter and Paul testify to the reality of Christian suffering, but then admonish us to stand and persevere during this experience. "If you suffer for doing good, and you are patient, then God is pleased. This is what you were called to do, because Christ suffered for you and gave you an example to follow. So you should do as he did" (1 Peter 2:20-21). Also, Job bears witness to the comfort we receive from God: "But God saves those who suffer through their suffering; he gets them to listen through their pain" (Job 36:15). But notice here that Job doesn't say this until after Satan takes everything from him—his family, his health, and all his possessions. Yet God blesses him again with all this and much more, perhaps because Job realizes that the most important thing he has is his relationship with God. Being humans, we will never fully understand the mind of God. He wants from us unconditional love, faithfulness, glory and praise, whether we know the reasons for our suffering or not.

Philip Yancey, in his book *Disappointment with God*, reminds us that "the Book of Job insists that . . . one person's faith can make a difference. There is a role for human beings, after all, and by fulfilling that role Job set a pattern for anyone who ever faced doubt or hardship. . . Job teaches that at the moment when faith is hardest and least likely, then faith is most needed."

Yancey further adds, "The book of Job gives no satisfying answers to the question 'Why?' Instead, it substitutes another question, 'To what end?' By remaining faithful to God through his trials, Job . . . helped abolish the very pain and unfairness of this world that he had protested so vigorously . . . Why the delay? Why does God let evil and pain so flagrantly exist, even thrive, on this planet? Why does he let us do slowly and blunderingly what he could do in an eye blink?" Yancey answers his own question, "He holds back for our sakes. Re-creation involves us; we are, in fact, at the center of his plan . . . The motive behind all human history is to develop us, not God. Our very existence announces to the powers in the universe that restoration is under way. Every act of faith by every one of the people of God is like the tolling bell, and a faith like Job's reverberates throughout the universe."

Faith, then, is surely a key ingredient of inner peace. When I listen to Laura's story and hear about similar situations, I feel their pain. Without holding on to God, what a truly miserable condition an individual would experience each day.

Transition

"Two people are better than one. If one falls down,
the other can help him up" (Ecclesiastes 4:9-10).

When diagnosed with multiple sclerosis in 1981 at the age of 27, I was working full-time as an orthodontic technician in Scottsdale, Arizona. In my ignorance, I remember leaving the doctor's office and asking my friend, Ann Prichard, "What is MS?" To my embarrassment, I must confess that I had no idea. She then went on to tell me what she understood about it.

Ann's husband passed away just three months before my finding out about this problem. My twin sister, Julie, had just married and moved to Houston, Texas. Consequently, Ann knew that I was looking for someone to share an apartment with. Her home was large. One of her sons lived with her while he attended college, but she asked if I would like to stay at her house. I thought, well, okay. Sure!

Ann is twenty years older than I am. Foolishly I was afraid that we would not have anything in common. Little did I know she would fulfill the saying, "A friend is there before you know it to lend a hand before you ask it and give you love just when you need it most." Ann was a schoolteacher who taught physics, chemistry, biology, and earth science, among other subjects. Her knowledge and professionalism always intimidated me a bit. She was so intelligent. I thought

47

she was too smart for me—that I couldn't even hold a conversation with her. So I thought, "Well, I'll just stay with her until I find someone else, and that shouldn't take too long." As it turned out, three months after I moved in with her I started having problems with my left leg. The problem progressed until all I could do was drag my leg behind me. Ann took me to an orthopedic surgeon who ran some tests, but at that time they had no definitive tests for MS. So, I had to take a CAT scan. From that, the doctors were certain that I had MS. The disease progressed so rapidly that before many months passed I could only work part-time. Within two years, I could only work one day a week. Eventually, my intellectual and motor skills diminished so drastically that I could no longer meet the demands of the job. Reluctantly, my employer relieved me of my duties. But he kept my health coverage in force for six months and gave me the complete Pension Profit Sharing Package that I would have accrued at my retirement.

During this painstaking transition in my life, God never failed to confirm his love and care for me. I am well aware of the fact that these circumstances could have given Satan an opportune moment to work his evil in my heart. Fortunately, God's power reflected his generous outpouring of love and support from my family, friends, and church.

His care further expressed itself by my being eligible quickly for Social Security disability benefits, followed by Medicare after a two-year interval. During this time I lived at the poverty level. Without all the expressions of love and care I received, I'm not sure where I would be today. However, it would be impossible – downright ungrateful on my part – for me not to see God's hand of love and care working in my life. It was another example of his all-knowing love guiding me and providing the stepping-stones down my path toward inner peace.

I want to tell this story about Ann. It's amazing how God works in our lives. She was a Godsend to me. And she said that I was the same to her. God knew that we both needed each other to get through our times of grief. I was there to take her mind off the loss of her husband. She was there to give me the support that I needed as my active life crumbled. Ann and I became great friends. Seventeen years later we are still great friends. She is such an inspiration to me. Ann is a mentor, counselor, and confidant. In the early days of our friendship and before MS slowed me down, we loved to go camping and hiking. She would come home from work on Fridays and say, "Hey! Do you want to go out to the lake, or go up to the mountains for the weekend?" And I'd say, "Sure!" She told me I was always ready because I just loved to be in the woods. As I've mentioned before, this was a special time when God put my life into his perspective, and I became focused on him. Doing this always resulted in strengthening the stepping-stones of inner peace. So Ann and I would throw everything into the van and take off.

We had some grand times together. Ann taught me much. I could ask her anything because she is so knowledgeable. She would answer all my questions. I would kid her because she always told me more than I wanted to know. I never remembered anything she told me anyway. I still don't.

We both enjoyed the same things. I loved earth science. Rocks and minerals fascinated me. I wanted to learn all that I could about nature. She was the perfect one to teach me. We went to Yosemite and hiked down the Grand Canyon to Havasupi Falls. What awesome displays of God's handiwork!

This poem I wrote is an example of how deeply God inspired and moved me during these experiences:

The Faces of Spring

Dawn's early mist hangs suspended above lush, green meadows,
While spring freshness brings jubilant life to butterflies as they
Dance from blossom to blossom.
Nearby, a swan's graceful glide is mirrored on a peaceful
Mountain lake. Sudden breezes whip the gentle water
Into excited ripples.
In the distance, lowering clouds announce an approaching storm
As the rumble of thunder reverberates
Off mighty canyon walls.
Wickedly, lightning flashes and signals the towering thunderheads
To erupt with relentless fury. In relief they release
Their long-awaited nourishment.
Cascading falls shout with glee
And fullness as they eagerly roar
Down majestic granite cliffs.
Man's wonder increases as each awakened fragrance excites his senses,
While spring explodes across his vision
And God reveals creation's glorious colors.

I had varying periods of relapse and remission. But there were times when I could hike. I didn't use a cane regularly until 1990. During one of my periods of remission, we hiked down the Grand Canyon with backpacks. That was a tough hike! I think it was 24 miles round trip. Twelve miles down, we camped at the bottom, along with friends who made the trip with us. We stayed three nights and four days hiking around in that breathtaking environment. Hiking out was something else. I didn't know if I was going to make it. Thankfully, we had our backpacks on mules. That turned out to be a big help.

In 1982, Ann had an opportunity to go to Alaska and teach in the Eskimo village, Nunapichuk, out in the tundra. There were no roads in. The only way to reach her destination was to fly on a bi-plane. She stayed there for a couple of years. Meanwhile, she let me stay in her home in Arizona to housesit it for her (She gave me quite a bit of leeway). One of her sons continued to live there also, so the two of us kept up with it.

While in Alaska, Ann met a polite man, Wayne Hanson, and they became good friends. A few years later, they married. Now Ann divides her home between Alaska and Arizona. How I cherish our friendship! We're convinced that God engineered it. She has done so much for me in countless ways, so the depth of my gratitude to her is immeasurable. Ann is a true blessing from God and responsible in many ways for helping me find inner peace. Just knowing good friends are there to support you gives you a feeling of security and contentment. Aristotle spoke truly when he said, "In poverty and other misfortunes of life, true friends are a sure refuge. The young they keep out of mischief; to the old they are a comfort and aid in their weakness; and those in the prime of life they incite to noble deeds."

I think Ann's generosity is best reflected in the Gospel account of Matthew 25:34-40, where Jesus established his criteria for entering into the heavenly portals:

> Then the King will say to those on his right, "Come, my Father has given you his blessing. Receive the kingdom God has prepared for you since the world was made. I was hungry, and you gave me food. I was thirsty, and you gave me something to drink. I was alone and from home, and you invited me into your house. I was without clothes, and you gave me something to wear. I was sick, and you cared for me. I was in prison, [was imprisoned within the confines of my disease,] and you visited me . . . I tell you the truth, anything you did for even the least of my people here, you also did for me."

Postscript

On March 30, 1999, some time after I wrote the words above, Ann lost her life in a head-on automobile collision near Payson, Arizona. So many people loved her. She always went out of her way to make family, friends, and strangers feel welcome and important. She greatly enriched my life and contributed immeasurably to the success of my quest for inner peace. I have been blessed with many wonderful friends. Without a doubt, Ann was truly the very best and most extraordinary friend of all. It is often said that to have even one friend such as this seldom happens—perhaps only once in a lifetime. I know that Ann is already in Heaven, waiting to continue our heavenly friendship for all eternity. So, my dear, lovely friend, I miss you terribly and am eagerly awaiting that breathless, glorious reunion!

Ann

> *Grief scrapes me raw inside*
> *My heart is weeping tears*
> *A lovely Christian's light has been extinguished*
> *But is now shining brilliantly in Heaven*
> *Our loss has made Heaven a brighter place*
> *Which makes our blessings there even more joyful*
> *Because Ann is waiting to greet us*
> *With her warm, friendly smile*

Since we are willing vessels, God will lead us and guide us in his direction. Sometimes that direction may not be the way we want to go. But when we just let him take over, he leads us to places and blessings we otherwise could not possibly imagine.

I don't know why we make it so hard on ourselves. We know that when we let God remain in charge, things work out for the best. We then move toward the development of inner peace. Part of the process is turning everything over to God. He longs to take care of us and bless us better than we ever expected.

God's Perfect Timing

"God never takes away except to give us back something better. It means we must be brave enough and determined enough to wait . . . because it often takes God time to turn a painful situation to good. We can embrace our pain and not resent it because a blessing is coming!"
—Ann Kiemel Anderson

y father died of kidney failure in 1983. He endured three years of dialysis procedures, hospitalizations, and then, during an operation, he died of a blood clot in his brain. I don't think I ever truly realized what Mom coped with. As a true nurse and loving wife, she tenderly cared for him until he passed away. It is never easy to lose a parent. At least I have some wonderful and happy memories of Daddy, as reflected in my poem about him:

Tackle Boxes, Little Girls, And Daddy

The twinkle in his eye told us,
This was a special day indeed.
Fishing pole supplied by smiling Mom,
With vain attempts restoring calm.

Little girls with starry eyes,
In hopes of catching many.
Undaunted by crisp morning chill,
Adventure lay over the next hill.

"How can you keep it?"
Lamented twin sister, Julie,
"It's just a little baby!
You're just a selfish meanie!"

Yet Judy, unmoved by guilt,
Turns pleading eyes toward Daddy.
After all! It was her very first catch.
To her there was no greater match.

But at end of day
When Dad cleaned all the fish,
Judy was feeling a little queasy,
For thoughts of eating weren't easy.

As the years rolled by,
Daddy taught us many sports.
Each day was very special to us
Because the family was his focus.

Bringing treats home from the bakery,
Or finding something new to build,
Looking for mushrooms in the woods nearby,
Always brought a sparkle to his eye.

Of all the activities we shared with Dad,
Without a doubt, only one was his favorite,
Not hunting, or golfing with a caddie,
But tackle boxes, little girls, and Daddy.

About one year after Daddy died, Mom moved to Arizona and stayed with me in Ann Prichard's home. She later found a place for herself and for her mother (my grandmother), who died three years later, at the age of 90.

Much has happened since those days back in 1987. I wrote the first words of this book. Julie and her husband Najel, while living in Houston, Texas, gave birth to a perfect little redheaded boy in 1988. Julie was relentless in pleading for Mom and me to join her in Houston. Mom and I made many visits and countless phone calls. In 1990, when we could stand the separation no longer, we made the inevitable move to Houston. I say this because I believe, without a doubt, that God brought us to a point that made it possible for us to let go of the situation where we were so comfortable. Then he engineered our migration to an exciting new life. But profound sadness awaited me after the move. Mom died of heart complications on June 27, 1991, not long after our move to Houston. Her passing still leaves a profound emptiness in my heart. I miss her so much. The pain from that loss still overwhelms me at times.

Losing Daddy was difficult for us, but we were prepared. Mom's death was totally unexpected. On Saturday night, May 6, 1991, neither one of us could sleep, so we got up, opened a window in the living room, and listened to the rain splattering on the leaves and the sidewalk. The following morning I got ready for church, but Mom said she wasn't feeling well. She said she would just stay home.

The storm knocked out our electricity during the night, so when Julie and Najel came to pick us up for church, we tried to persuade Mom to go home with them after services that morning. I knew I was going to church because, in the Houston heat and humidity, we didn't have any air conditioning. Also, without power, we did not have any way to prepare meals. We practically dragged Mom, kicking and screaming, out the door. She just wanted to go back to bed and sleep.

Mom did sleep during lunch at Julie and Najel's. When she got up, she told us that she had already taken nitroglycerin but didn't feel any better. This was our first clue that she suspected heart problems. She asked me if she should take another pill. I told her that she was the nurse and that I didn't know. Thinking back on that now, I just want to kick myself. My words sounded so cruel. And then I told her that if she thought it was her heart, maybe we should call an ambulance. She really didn't want to do that. So she just took another pill and went back to bed. Thirty minutes later she was back up, feeling much worse. While she lay on the sofa, Najel called the paramedics. My little nephew Wesley was just three at the time. He was confused and frightened to see Grandma not feeling good and in pain. He went over to her and gave her a bottle of vitamins, telling her that they would help her feel better. Mom just closed her eyes, shook her head, and started moaning.

About that time the ambulance arrived. Three paramedics came in and immediately began to monitor Mom's heart and take her vital signs. They informed us that she should go to the hospital and wanted one of us to ride with them. I volunteered, but they wouldn't let me ride in the back with her. I had to sit up front in the passenger seat. We took off with sirens wailing and lights flashing. That was some ride! Traffic pulled in front of us, and some refused to get out of the way. I had a newfound respect and appreciation for ambulance drivers after that.

Mom remained in the hospital for seven weeks. We never dreamed that she would not leave the hospital alive. Her stay was quite an ordeal. They administered the usual barrage of tests. After several weeks she was in so much pain you could hear her begging for painkillers all the way down the hall. We knew that wasn't like Mom. They ended doing emergency gallbladder surgery, during which she suffered several heart attacks. The doctors told us that she had died, but they revived her two or three times. She had a living will that made what happened afterwards seem unnecessary and cruel punishment.

Mom's brother and sister-in-law from Arizona, John and Esther Bowman, drove to Texas when they heard that Mom was sick. Aunt Esther had been stoically suffering from Parkinson's disease for years, and still is. She has miraculously and gratefully found an avenue of relief for her continually shaking hands. To her doctor's amazement, she discovered that while crocheting, her tremors stop. This truly is astounding! Her work is so exquisite that her tablecloths are in constant demand. To complete projects of this size, however, takes her at least six months and sometimes longer.

Long ago I lost count of the times she spoke of her desire to be an encourager. When she quotes, "The Lord is my Shepherd, I shall not want," she says that whatever comes, she will try to go with it. I was glad that she and Uncle John came to Texas to be with Mom. Their cheerful spirits were a blessing to us.

While visiting with Mom in the hospital, Uncle John was himself admitted to the emergency room because of recurring back pain that made him unable to straighten up. He ended staying there for a few weeks. If there are true earthly saints, I believe Mom and Uncle John qualify.

Uncle John is such a dear. It breaks my heart to report that in April of 1998 he was diagnosed as having terminal pancreatic cancer, with six months to one year to live. Within a month, however, he was admitted to Hospice care for complications of blood clots in his right leg. He also had pneumonia, a spot on his lung, and was coughing up blood. The cancer had spread throughout his body. At that point, Julie and I decided to go to Arizona so that we could be there for Uncle John and Aunt Esther. They had been such strength for us at the time of Mom's death. We wanted to be there for them in whatever ways they needed. Family is so important. Uncle John passed away on June 27 that year. In a strange sort of way I found comfort in the fact that he died on the same date Mom did seven years earlier. It was almost as if he willed himself to die on that precise date. I even predicted to David and Julie that Uncle John was waiting to die on that day. He and Mom had been so close. Shortly after he learned about his terminal cancer, he looked up toward heaven and said, "Roberta, I'll see you soon!"

The day before Uncle John passed away, several members of the family were at his bedside. While he was comatose, suddenly he stretched out his arms. Then, bringing his hands toward his face, he folded them together, as if he were in prayer, and remained like that for several minutes. The atmosphere in the room was electric. I had the excited feeling that he was not only speaking to God, but that he also saw God. We all just held our breaths. He looked like a little boy praying. That will always be a cherished memory of mine. He was such a dear, gentle man. I wrote the following poem for him shortly after learning of his cancer:

A Gentle, Quiet Man

Abiding faith describes him.
Humbly serving on bended knee.
A man after God's own heart.
Like David, his life a melody.

Tenderness and love he gives
To many lonely souls.
Teaching countless searching hearts
The promise God bestows.
A gentle, quiet man,
With wisdom he gives life,
Instilling strength and peace,
Dissolving fearful strife.

Created in God's own image,
Uncle John mirrors Christ's wondrous traits.
Dearly loved by so many people,
Especially to me – he is an earthly "saint."

I want to return for a moment to my story of Mom's death. Uncle John was in the hospital for several weeks with recurring back pain. Every time we visited Mom you could see the questions in her eyes – no doubt wondering where Uncle John was. We were reluctant to tell her, fearing it would weaken her even more. When Uncle John recovered, he and I received a request to sign papers releasing her from life support. Mom had a living will. We knew from the will, and from conversations with Mom that she wanted us to sign the papers. I will never forget Uncle John telling her what was about to happen. We were not sure she was lucid. It seemed that she was. Uncle John held one of her hands and gently brushed her hair away from her face. I held her other hand. While he talked to her, she looked at him with the most loving, trusting expression I have ever seen. He was crying, and I was crying. Mom looked so childlike in her trusting. She kept nodding and smiling and squeezing our hands. A few days later, she died.

Her heart weakened so that the remainder of her vital organs began shutting down one by one. Her kidneys shut down. They put her on dialysis, which didn't help. After a few days, they took her off it. They put her on a breathing machine when her lungs began filling with fluid. This was really frustrating for all of us because she kept trying desperately to tell us something, but she had a large tube in her throat. The result was virtually zero communication. We asked her many questions, but all she could do was shake her head no. We wrote things on paper and tried to get her to write something. That didn't work either. We never did find out what she was trying to tell us. (Uncle John told us shortly before he died that when he got to Heaven, he was going to ask Mom what she tried to say to us.)

Eventually gangrene set in. The nurses tied her hands down so that she couldn't see what they looked like. It was horrible! Her hands, feet, and legs turned black and just shriveled up. They looked like prunes. She also developed huge blisters that would burst and ooze. The nurses wouldn't let us touch her because the gangrene was contagious. I still tried to find an area where I could touch her. It seemed so unfair. She had devoted 33 years of her life as a nurse taking care of others. To see her in that condition just broke my heart.

You might be asking yourself, "After watching your mother die in that manner, how could you find inner peace?" Well, to be honest, it hasn't been easy. But, yes, I have found it. My peace comes with the belief that she is at peace now and is no longer suffering. She went into a coma from which she never revived. Though it has been seven years since she died, it still seems like yesterday. (I'm crying as I write this.) She did meet David, my fiancé, and just loved him. My regret is that she didn't live long enough to see me finally married. She worried so much about my care. I like to believe she knows that I am happy and taken care of like a queen. Mom truly was a treasure. I pray that my life mirrors the qualities of Jesus as sweetly and devotedly as her life did. What an honor and a blessing to call her my mother. To honor her, I wrote:

Mom

Family treasures sketched in time,
Countless memories etched in minds,
Loving words and gentle hands,
That soothe the pain – Mom understands.

Always there with words of cheer,
Knowing that laughter dries the tears,
A nurse for life she proved to be,
Hospital patients, and family.

Others first seemed to be her rule,
Sweet humility adhered like glue,
My hero she will always be,
Teaching love and charity.

Birthday cakes and treasure hunts,
Football games and field goal punts,
Her specialty was love and support,
Serene demeanor – reflecting calm retort.

So dear, sweet, Mom,
My lifelong balm,
There is no earthly measure,
To you – our family treasure.

I'm so glad Mom was alive when I met David and that she was a part of our amazing courtship. It all began when Mom and I moved from Arizona to Texas in March of 1990. We started attending church where my sister and her family were members. I was sitting in my chair reading the bulletin, waiting for the services to start. Julie, Najel, and Mom had gone to pick up Wesley from his class. There were three empty chairs to my left. About that time, my family returned and sat on my right side. The church was filling rapidly, but the three chairs beside me remained empty. Then my attention was drawn to a well-dressed man making his way to the chair

right next to me. Simultaneously he tried politely to maneu-
ver over my ill-placed cane. Being the perfect gentleman, he
stepped over my cane. I was embarrassed because he was so
gracious about the whole procedure.

I noticed that he didn't have a hymnal, but in my eagerness to share mine with him, I dropped it in his lap. Of
course, that was a good start! We started laughing and then
tried to compose ourselves for the song service. The
preacher at the time was excellent, but I have to admit that I
was more aware of this good-looking man next to me than I
was of the sermon that day. I was strongly attracted to him
and really hoped to see him again.

When I realized he was from The Woodlands, where
Mom and I now lived, I was elated. His address was just down
the street from us, less than five minutes away. After services
we talked again. People will correctly tell you that I am not a
forward person, but I wanted him to know that I was interested in him without scaring him off. Because he was visiting
the church that day, I asked him if we would see him the
following week. Taken aback and he said, "Well, yes!" We've
laughed about that since then. We both returned the next
Sunday, but didn't see each other.

Later, I told my sister that I would give him two weeks and
then I would call him. It's not like me to be so assertive.
Nevertheless, Mom, Julie, and I drove down David's street to
check out where he lived. All the houses around it were big two
and three-story homes. His house looked like it was one story,
and I thought, "That's great. I won't have to climb any stairs."
And I had the most calm, peaceful feeling come over me. I just
knew that David and I would marry. I even went so far as to say,
"I'm going to live there." This comment, of course, led Julie
and Mom to exchange skeptical glances, roll their eyes, and say,
"Yeah! Right!" Then they looked at me as though I had grown
an extra nose or something. But I just knew.

I said I'd give him two weeks. A week and a half later I got
a call. I didn't recognize his voice at first. He said, "I don't
know if you remember me or not. This is David Glover. I met
you at church a few Sundays ago." I said, "Oh, yes! I do!" He

then asked, "I don't want to be too bold here, but I wondered if you would like to go out to dinner Saturday night." We've laughed about this because I didn't want him to think I was too eager, but of course, I was. I paused a little bit (his version is that it was forever) and then I said, "Yes! I would love to!" He had not expected me to say "yes" because he didn't know if I was dating.

When I said, "yes," he began fumbling around for something to say because he wasn't prepared for it. We went out to eat and, to my astonishment, I learned that he already knew about my multiple sclerosis, and yet, he still was interested in me – as a person. I was just dumbfounded. Sitting across from me was the man of my dreams, treating me like I was a queen. It has been a fairy tale story ever since.

E. Havermann suggests, "Perhaps true love can best be recognized by the fact that it thrives under circumstances which would blast anything else into small pieces." David and I are convinced beyond any doubt that God engineered our meeting. It was a perfect time for this to happen. I'll never regret refusing to "just settle" for other men. I'd had other opportunities in the past, but never felt they were right. I always felt I would know in my heart when I met the right person. And I did know when I met David that he was the one.

On our first date I found out that he was vice president of a global petrochemical storage company. But I wasn't intimidated, which is quite amazing for me. We felt like we had known each other all our lives. We've been friends from the start.

I wrote these words in 1998. We were married in November of 1991 after a year and a half of dating. I was eager to marry sooner, but he wanted to give us time to get to know each other better. He still gets just as excited telling our story as I do. I'm overwhelmed at the ways God has blessed me all my life, especially in preparing this wonderful man for me to marry. I think about this often and become overwhelmed to the point of tears, because God is such a provider of wonderful things.

Seeing his guidance in my life keeps my faith alive and

fills me with peace. I pray for God to help me never to limit his extraordinary blessings or doubt his decisions. He took my Mom and gave me David to love and care for me after her departure. God's timing is always perfect.

Chapter 6

The Power of Perseverance

"Should we take only good things from God and not trouble" (Job 2:10)?

In the January following our November wedding, David was playing his customary style of tennis. He played full speed ahead, trying to make the last point, even if it killed him. It almost did. He had a heart attack. I was at home when I got the call from his tennis partner. He told me that David had collapsed and the paramedics were about to take him to the hospital. He is a diabetic, so all of us thought he had a reaction to his medicine. David wanted me to bring his medicine to him, thinking that he might have forgotten something. I immediately gathered all his medicine and drove to be with him at April Sound, Texas, about thirty minutes away. That was the longest drive of my life. When I arrived at the club, the ambulance met me leaving with lights flashing and siren wailing. David's tennis partner stopped me and told me to follow him. The paramedics said that David had suffered a heart attack, and that they were taking him to the nearest hospital about 15 minutes away.

When I arrived at the Emergency Room, I found David tied down on the gurney and in a neck brace. He looked like a turnip. All the blood had drained to his chin. The upper two-thirds of his face was white. The lower part was beet-red. His teeth chattered. His lips trembled. When I saw him in that condition, my heart broke. He looked at me and said, "I'm sorry, Babe. They say I'm having a heart attack." I could tell he was afraid but was trying to be brave about it. He was so cold and shaking. His father had died of a massive heart attack in his late 50's. I knew David had to be thinking about that. The doctor and nurse asked me to leave because they were going to give him a clot-buster shot. When I returned, David informed me that they had given him two shots.

The following evening, we transferred him by ambulance to Methodist Hospital in the Medical Center of Houston. I rode along. He joked with the paramedics all the way. I will say this about my wonderful husband – he always tries to find humor in everything. How true it is that "a happy heart is like good medicine" (Proverbs 17:22).

David told me later that when the paramedics arrived at April Sound, they removed his warm-up jacket by cutting it off. This did not set well with David. He went on to inform them of the value of the garment and wanted to know if that expense would be deducted from his bill. Meanwhile, the paramedics were trying to get a reading on his pulse. When this failed, David's amazing remark was, "I know I'm not dead because I know I'm going to heaven, and I don't expect to see you people there with me." They chuckled, of course. Their next taste of his humor was when they informed him that he was having a heart attack. When they asked him which hospital he wanted admittance to, he asked them how bad his condition was. They responded resoundingly with the frightening words, "It's bad!" His smiling response was to say, "How about the closest one?" As he related this story to me, I had to keep in mind that he was joking around with them while in a life-threatening situation. Such is his endearing disposition.

David's stay was traumatic. I'm glad I could be there for him as he has been for me. He's doing well now, and I am grateful to God for his recovery.

Though weary, love is not tired;
Though pressed, it is not straitened;
Though alarmed, it is not confounded.
Love securely passes through all.
–Thomas á Kempis

The medical saga of my past two decades is daunting. First, the diagnosis of Multiple Sclerosis along with all its accompanying debilitation hit me. I've become far more familiar with hospitals than I care to be. I've tried to remember how many hospital stays I've had since my move to The Woodlands in 1990, but I don't remember for sure. There were many though, either for my Multiple Sclerosis or for various surgeries.

The first surgery I recall probably occurred in 1992, several months after David and I were married. I needed a hysterectomy because of endometriosis, which proved to be painful, as any woman who suffers with this condition would heartily agree. Recovery took several weeks. Another stay began on April 1, 1993, when I was admitted to Methodist Hospital in Houston. I lapsed into a rapid exacerbation of Multiple Sclerosis so severe that my entire left side became paralyzed. This caused me to fall several times in our home. I would start laughing when I couldn't get up and would call my husband in the next room to come and help me (a little "tongue-in-cheek" here). "Honey! I've fallen and I can' t get up!" Okay, it wasn't funny.

Before long it truly was not a laughing matter. Again I had to enter the hospital with an uncertain prognosis. I have learned a valuable lesson while dealing with this persistent disease. Live one day at a time. There is no other way. I've tried borrowing trouble. Humanly speaking, we have a tendency to seek and expect the worst-case scenarios (you know, the Murphy's Law syndrome). Such thinking only adds to our hardships. We all know this to be true, yet we still continue to borrow trouble. Jesus tells us in Matthew 6:34 that we shouldn't worry about tomorrow because each day has plenty of problems of its own. That's my point. It is a wonderful blessing to know that God was (and still is) with me each day. There is no need to worry about tomorrow. Realizing this kept the flames of inner peace steadily burning in my soul during some of my darkest days.

To begin with, I was admitted to the Intensive Care Unit for powerful doses of Lidacain (a painkilling medication) administered intravenously. Because it was potentially lethal, they monitored my vital signs around the clock. Frequent Electrocardiograms (EKG) was one way of monitoring. They detect irregularities in the heart, a possible side effect of Lidacain. Another reason for this hospitalization was to let me take Methilprednisalone (steroid) treatments. High doses of this for five days are beneficial in slowing the progression of MS in many patients.

Upon completion of those treatments, I was moved to a private room. The paralysis was still present, so the next step was physical therapy twice a day. Those sessions were more interesting than you might imagine. They proved to be a source of mental and emotional healing. They diverted my attention away from myself, making me focus on other patients. Some of them were much more traumatized than I was. I learned much in those days about the human need for interrelatedness. In the sense of human suffering, we were together, yet individually trying to overcome personal trials to the best of our ability. Also, we shared common goals. Usually I observed in others a very strong will and desire to overcome. But our bodies were often painfully weak. Pushed to the limit, we seemed too exhausted to continue. Nevertheless, in all of this, we achieved success, with many heartwarming sighs of relief and smiles of gratitude expressed by all around. Max Lucado's thoughts in his book, *He Still Moves Stones*, fuel the fires of inner peace within me:

They are historic moments in which a real God met real pain so we could answer the question, "Where is God when I hurt?"

How does God react to dashed hopes? Read the story of Jairus. How does the Father feel about those who are ill? Stand with him at the pool of Bethesda. Do you long for God to speak to your lonely heart? Then listen as he speaks to the Emmaus-bound disciples. What is God's word for the shameful? Watch as his finger draws in the dirt of the Jerusalem courtyard.

He's not doing it just for them. He's doing it for you . . .

I know there used to be a stone in front of a tomb. And I know it was moved. And I also know that there are stones in your path. Stones that trip and stones that trap. Stones too big for you.

Please remember, the goal of these stories is not to help us look back with amazement, but forward with faith. The God who spoke still speaks. The God who forgave still forgives. The God who came still comes. He comes into our world. He comes to do what you can't. He comes to move the stones you can't budge.

Stones are no match for God. Not then and not now. He still moves stones.

My health improved. My paralysis went away. But severe tremors developed in my left arm and side. At times it resembles Parkinson's disease. After a month of treatments, I was released from the hospital, although only partial improvement had been accomplished. I realize that the medical profession can do only so much to help me until a cure for MS is found. I am pleased that I at least regained the use of the left side of my body, however limited that may be.

Some of you have endured longer stays in the hospital. You may think that my story is no big deal. I'm inclined to agree with you. May I make a suggestion to you? Each person has his/her own set of trials that are as unique and intimate as we are to God. God teaches me in suffering not to base other's pain and experiences on my unique perspective of these trials. My pain threshold and tolerance are high. In these hardships God taught me to respect the fact that every person is unique and special in his eyes. Therefore, it is my responsibility as a member of the human race to attempt to empathize with others in their times of trial, whatever form that may take.

A major treatment for MS is Betaseron (Interferon beta-1b). This was approved by the FDA after many years of clinical testing and is administered every other day by injections into the subcutaneous tissue. Specific areas are charted, those being thighs, back of arms, abdomen, and the buttocks. Proper administration of this drug proved to reduce the frequency of relapses (exacerbations) for patients suffering with relapsing-remitting MS. Other exciting factors involved were that the periods between exacerbations lasted longer. Manifestations also showed less severe relapses. It thrilled me to have the opportunity to use this drug. I might add, though, that it was not without significant side effects. In my case, after nine months an alarming adverse reaction developed. All the signs of coming trouble were there for months. When I went to see my neurologist for regular checkups, I frequently complained about the tenderness and severe pain I experienced in the injection sites. The usual response from the medical community was a polite nodding of heads, scribbling of notes, and the added agreement, "Yes, Mrs. Glover, we're sure this is extremely uncomfortable for you." Then I would hear the usual litany of reasons why I should press on, despite pain. I began to feel that I was just not tough enough. "No pain! No gain!" they say. Well, I am the first to agree with that. That has been my motto and behavior as far back as I can remember.

On Christmas of 1994, for example, when David and I were visiting family and friends in Mesa, Arizona, I got a chance to prove this. I had been diligently taking the Betaseron injections since March that year. Christmas morning dawned bright and cheerful, with expectations of a wonderful day visiting with family and friends. Unfortunately, I awoke experiencing extreme abdominal pain. It was so severe that I was literally doubled over. I thought that I was having appendicitis. David knows that I can endure a great amount of pain and discomfort, but he took one look at me and realized this was serious. We drove directly to the nearest hospital Emergency Room where I was admitted immediately. After many questions about my medical history, a series of x-rays, and much punching and probing, I was finally diagnosed with Necrotizing Subcutaneous Infection. This is a serious infection that causes the fatty tissue to die. If this condition worsens, gangrene may develop. Inwardly, I groaned, thinking, "That's just great!" The injections I had diligently administered for the last nine months were seriously harming me. The doctor released me with a prescription for antibiotics and strongly advised me to see my neurologist when I returned to Houston. Well, that was a "no brainer," I thought. (Obviously, that remark reflects my disparaging observations and pent-up emotions in dealing with this newfound hardship.)

After discussing with my neurologist the unsettling events that had happened in Arizona, I decided to stop the Betaseron therapy. He wasn't thrilled about this decision, but he told me it was really up to me. You better believe it was. And I did stop the treatments, with no regrets. In fairness to this drug, it has helped, and continues to help, many patients with MS. Unfortunately, my body rejected this chemical substance. Even now, long after I stopped the medication, those injection sites are extremely tender to the touch. Subsequent surgeries revealed the massive extent of the damage I suffered while attempting this therapy.

During the Interferon treatment, I noticed a knot, or lump, in my upper left arm and pointed it out to various doctors. Ultimately, they sent me to a general surgeon who scheduled me for immediate surgery to remove the lump and find out what kind of tumor it was. While removing the tumor, which proved to be a fatty tissue tumor, he discovered extensive fatty tissue necrosis. He admitted his astonishment and alarm at the extensive destruction of tissue. Realizing the seriousness of this infection, he set about digging out (his words) all the infection he could find. When he completed this task, he confirmed that he was successful in getting it all. I was grateful to hear that news.

Several weeks later, however, after the scar had healed, I was still experiencing a great deal of pain in that area. With each new day, the range of motion in that arm became increasingly limited. I would wake up in the middle of the night screaming at the top of my lungs from the pain. To this day, I don't know how David slept through the ordeal. He probably was afraid to wake up and discover a new set of problems. I just could not bear the excruciating pain. My whole arm felt like it would crumble into a million pieces with the slightest pressure against it. If an illuminated sign had been attached to my body, the message flashing (in large, bright red letters) would have read PAIN! PAIN! PAIN! Not only was the pain related to the latest surgery, but also a newfound pain stabbed me in my left shoulder. I knew I must deal with this new pain.

My latest neurologist suspected that the problem might be a frozen shoulder and recommended that I see an orthopedic surgeon. A few days later, David and I visited with a highly recommended surgeon in the Houston Medical Center. He confirmed my neurologist's assessment. I had adhesive capsulitis, or in layman's terms, a frozen shoulder. When this happens, the range of motion in the effected extremity is severely limited and extremely painful because of joint inflammation. There is pain because the capsulitis membrane surrounding the shoulder adheres itself to the bone. Forced manipulation therefore becomes mandatory. This was done when my surgeon rotated my shoulder through all the manipulations while I was unconscious. He told us later that it snapped, crackled, and popped (just like Rice Krispies) because of the capsulitis breaking up through all the ranges of motion. It was something I could not possibly have accomplished on my own because of the pain and severity of the problem. Follow-up treatment included anti-inflammatory medication and outpatient physical therapy. I also had to do exercises at home on a motorized chair specifically designed for forced manipulation.

After the first three weeks of physical therapy, my progress literally came to a screaming halt. My therapist and I were both frustrated and puzzled. The pain was not coming from my shoulder. To my dismay and alarm, it came from the scar area where I had the earlier surgery for the tumor and necrosis.

Returning to my surgeon for follow-up analysis of physical therapy and progress, I informed him of the latest turn of events. He had received word from my physical therapist about what was happening so he wasn't surprised to hear my confirmation of these discouraging developments.

Armed with this news, he again did surgery, although this time it was far more invasive. Fearing that the necrosis and tumor surgery I had undergone a few months before were the underlying problems, he set about reopening the scar. Validating his consternation, the scar tissue adhered through the muscle. It was on the verge of attaching itself to the bone extending all the way up through my shoulder. To his dismay, he discovered more necrosis.

As I mentioned earlier, this is an extremely life-threatening infection because of the gangrene that may develop if the dead tissue remains. Aware of this, the surgeon dug out all the effected area, removed the previous scar, closed it up, and gave me a new scar. Then he did surgery on my shoulder for the adhesive capsulitis. I went home with lots of painkillers and anti-inflammatory medicine. I continued home exercises and therapy. Also, I continued more outpatient therapy. I'm happy to say that this worked. But I must continue my home exercises at least four to five times a week for the rest of my life. Otherwise my shoulder will freeze up again. Although I have faith and trust in God's plan for me, at times I become discouraged. In this poem I confess those feelings:

Battle Fatigue

Dear Heavenly Father, I humbly ask for strength to continue
Dealing with this daily pain. I must confess that I am growing tired
Of the struggle and find My thoughts longing for heaven – to be with you,
Selfishly, for reasons of being free of pain.

Well-meaning friends and family comment frequently of how
Much they admire how bravely I am dealing with MS
And the various surgeries I've had. I don't think of
Myself as being brave. I just try to survive to the
Best of my ability, strength and will.

Lately, I've noticed that my will is losing ground to
Resignation and hopelessness. I've always been
Optimistic that I could handle this well – no matter what!
And I know Father that you are with me, and care
About what happens to me. I couldn't have come
This far without you!

Yet, now I find myself tired of the fight – more than ever!
As I read over this, I'm reminded of the battles Jesus had,
And of his pleas for deliverance. Yet he never took his
Eyes or hopes off you. O, for a portion of his strength
And faith. It is my prayer that my life will honor you, in spite,
Or even because of, this daily pain that I must endure.

I just wish that I could be healthy for David, the wonderful
Husband you have given me. Yet, I have one health problem
Right after the other – many things to deal with at the same
Time. I'm beginning to sound like a wimp, even complaining to
You. But this cannot be good for him. Please, Father! Don't
Let my problems weaken his health and cause him undue stress.
I want to hold on to hope! It's just that I am so tired!

I like the way Ruth Bell Graham expresses the rest and comfort she finds by going to God in prayer:

Lord, when my soul is weary and my heart is tired and sore,

And I have that failing feeling that I can't take it anymore,

Then let me know the freshening found in simple, childlike prayer,

When the kneeling soul knows surely that a listening Lord is there.

Incidentally, I want to reiterate the value inner peace has played throughout the extraordinary events of my life. God is amazingly patient with me. This knowledge serves to fuel my determination to walk with him daily. How could I do anything less? He has proved that he will not leave me alone and defenseless against the attacks of Satan.

Forgive me for "preaching," as my husband says I am prone to do. However, in my observation of human nature, I am astonished at man's penchant for taking God's grace for granted, perhaps even tripping over his eagerness to mock that amazing grace. How it must break his heart. The prophet Isaiah expressed it, "When they suffered, he suffered also" (63:9). How dare we? Perhaps because of elusive expectations, dashed hopes, unrealized dreams. And all the while Satan smiles. Again, how dare we? And what a frightening picture. Not only is it a picture, it is also a reality.

The only way inner peace is available to me, or to anyone, is through an abiding relationship with God. In this I have found that his love cradles and envelops my heart and soul with the warmth of his peace and faithfulness. The fruit of his Spirit is peace (Galatians 5:22).

Satan puts me to the test, minute by minute, even as I type these words. It has taken me a week (4-5 hours a day) to type seven pages. The reason is because I can only use one finger due to these frustrating and aggravating tremors. But I am determined to finish this book. I have the words, *"don't ever give up,"* taped above my computer screen. Believe me, there have been many times when I listened to Satan's voice instead of God's and wanted to give up on this book. But God's Holy Spirit keeps me going. And I press on.

Nevertheless, I do have to take breaks because my arm and hand get so tired, which causes weakness and spasticity. When this happens, I am left with two non-functioning arms. I must confess that this is the most daunting and frightening exacerbation of all because then I am really helpless. It is so severe at times that it drastically limits my ability to do normal daily functions. David and I jokingly remark that if we needed anything mixed well, all we have to do is put it in my left hand and . . .*voila!* David's sense of humor has been a true blessing in helping me deal with the frustrations of MS.

I know that my sense of hopelessness is a tool Satan uses to slow God's work. Since I prayerfully, with faith, listen to God and just press on, then his voice and his work come alive in my mind. Thus, he enables my hand and arm to complete this work. Consequently, I give God the glory and credit that he and I have come this far. I know that he will enable me to finish this work that he has begun in me. I joyfully exclaim, as Paul did, "I don't care about my own life. The most important thing is that I complete my mission, the work that the Lord Jesus gave me – to tell people the Good News about God's grace" (Acts 20:24).

Another back surgery is looming on the horizon, although I'm really not sure if I will give the green light to this one. I've had this surgery before in Arizona. It will involve repair of a past surgery for a herniated disk in the lumbar region of the vertebra. Also, a surgery on two new herniated disks in the thoracic region of the vertebra. Apparently, this damage is significant enough to warrant extensive repairs, involving the insertion of pins and other measures to put me back together.

I've had pain there some time. It began during my Arizona years. After many x-rays, doctors learned that I had arthritis in that area, so I periodically received cortisone injections directly into the disc area. This gave me almost instant relief that lasted for several months. I only begged for these three or four times, although I would have welcomed many more. But because it isn't advisable to keep taking this drug, I reluctantly endured the pain.

After these recent discoveries of two new herniated disks in

1997, the orthopedic surgeon in the Houston Medical Center exclaimed, with a touch of consternation and alarm, "What have you been doing to you back?" I honestly replied, "I don't know."

Before my MS surfaced I lived an active life. Because I was highly competitive, I loved challenging others and myself in sports. I competed in any sport – basketball, softball, hockey, tennis, racquetball, volleyball, hiking, climbing, ice skating, snow skiing, water skiing, bowling – just to name a few. My ten years of work as a dental and orthodontic technician likely put some additional strain on my back. I enjoyed these activities tremendously. But my enthusiasm evidently proved to be my undoing. Because I was in such good health, I believed I was invincible. During my senior year of high school, I was awarded The President of the United States Gold Seal Award for physical fitness.

So to answer the orthopedic surgeon's question regarding my back, I suppose I quite literally abused it. (Though I still miss being able to participate physically in those activities, I have discovered new interests that have proven to be much more fulfilling, especially as they relate to my service to God.) I enjoy visiting with the elderly either by telephone, taking them to lunch, going to their homes or to church gatherings, and, of course, writing poetry or nonfiction works such as this book.

Despite the supposed benefits that surgery offers me, and the remarkable feats I know surgeons can accomplish, I am a bit of a skeptic. I no longer believe that doctors can fix everything. Forgive me, doctors. Perhaps the entire trauma I have endured has predisposed me to a darkening opinion of our much-needed medical establishment. There will always be a few in the medical profession (as in all professions) who dishonor and blacken the profession they represent. While good doctors have blessed me with their wisdom and skills, still I must report that like the lady who came to Jesus for healing, I have "suffered much at the hands of many physicians."

I should mention that my twin sister, Julie, has chronic fatigue syndrome and has suffered with this devastating disease since 1982. We are heartbroken, but at least she does not have Multiple Sclerosis or Lupus, which were at first suspected. Julie is so sweet and unselfish in giving of her time and energy for others. I could not possibly express how dear she is to me. She is such a special sister and friend. I do not believe there is anything she would not do for me (except things that are above the laws of the land and God's laws, of course). She is so much like Mom in that she has such a tender, loving, and compassionate heart. She has told me many stories about times when she helped lost and lonely people, and animals also. Often these escapades resulted in hilarious rescues but also in happy endings.

This doesn't mean that I don't long, as she does, for those days without illness or pain. It's just that, as I mentioned earlier, it is harder to watch a loved one suffer than to suffer yourself. I admire Julie because she still reaches out to help others. She volunteers to help with her church card ministry, sending some fifty cards every week to members and others who need encouragement. She perseveres and finds a great measure of inner peace and fulfillment in putting her efforts into positive actions and thoughts.

One incredible experience happened not long ago to show me that God is not finished with me yet. I pause, now, because I want to reveal the circumstances that prompted the writing of this book. Yet, I'm hesitant. I don't know whether to speak boldly about this event or just to cherish it in my own private thoughts. However, the event itself was incredibly bold, so I feel compelled to share it. The pain from Multiple Sclerosis and from my back surgery became increasingly unbearable. I mention this, but I must admit that I don't know if it played a factor in this extraordinary tale. Whatever the reason, on that night, I went to bed as usual but awoke in a most unusual way.

To hear me tell it, even to my own ears, sounds preposterous, but I believe this truly did happen. Like the man described in 2 Corinthians 12:1-4, I don't know whether I was in the body or out of it. To me it seemed as though it was more my thoughts that were traveling through space (the heavens?) than my body. I honestly don't know. I (in whatever form) was traveling through space. I was not in a tunnel. I was literally floating past heavenly stars. I moved toward some astonishingly vivid lights. I knew it was Heaven!

I remember being so excited because I was about to see God and Jesus and just couldn't wait to be with my family and friends and the holy patriarchs. (These thoughts were flying whether my body was or not). I discovered it wasn't a "light" at the end of the tunnel. It was a real city with very high walls. But just as I was about to enter, I heard a voice. I knew, without a doubt, that it was God. The voice said, "Not yet, Judy." Immediately I woke up. My heart was pounding hard. I mean literally racing.

The sights throughout this experience, and my feelings afterwards, were incredible. I have never reached that degree of joy or sorrow before or since. The letdown, when I realized that God had sent me back to earth, was simply devastating. I sobbed. The disappointment was overwhelming. I questioned, "Why? Why did he send me back? Was there something I had not done for him?" From that experience, I was inspired and compelled to write this book.

This poem is perhaps an appropriate summation of my life and this book:

Hope

Through years of sorrow, triumph, and joy,
Your wakening Spirit is there to employ.
Your wisdom and guidance at close of day,
With little persuasion, I'm now led to say.

Whenever I'm lonely and silently weep,
You tenderly ease me, and soon I have peace.
Whenever I'm frightened and filled with despair,
You gently remind me that you're always there.

Whenever I'm hurting with sorrow and grief,
And cry out in pain for sudden relief,
Your love and compassion are not out of reach,
With patience you guide me and show me release.

The worst pain of all is when those we hold dear,
Are burdened with sorrow, confusion, and fear.
With no words of comfort and failure to cheer,
The days are stretched lonely, discernment unclear.

Each day I am learning through struggle and strife,
It will never be easy – this frail human life.
For why should we not suffer and bend beneath the loads?
Did Your Son not also? Yet, his faith – never cold.

I know you hurt with us, sharing our grief,
And someday we'll join you in Heavenly peace.
Till then, bear with us and help us to stand.
Encourage our journey with your knowing hand.

Chapter 7

Developing Inner Peace

"When you have many kinds of troubles, you should be full of joy, because you know that these troubles test your faith, and this will give you patience" (James 1:2-3).

Inner peace. Webster defines inner as pertaining to the mind or spirit and peace as freedom from fears or worries, a calm, quiet tranquility. When I reflect on my personal journey to inner peace, the image that comes to my mind is tranquil waters gently lapping against my troubled soul. This mind picture creates an aura of serene grace in my heart, grace that radiates as contentment and love. Is this inner tranquility really possible, or is it something that always is just out of our reach? Maybe you feel that it is not in the picture at all, but is instead an illusion, an abstract theory, or an elusive desire impossible to realize in this life.

In his book, *The Power of Positive Thinking*, Norman Vincent Peale emphasizes the need to visualize what we pray for. If we believe that what we pray for is for the good of mankind, then we will receive it. What a comforting thought, especially when applied to inner peace. What is important and pleasing to God is that we seek and hold on to him for guidance and strength when we pray. Our faithfulness to God is what he most wants from us. Inner peace hinges on our continuous recognition of God as Lord and Master of our lives.

To some this may seem like a trite remark, and they may respond, "Of course, we must spend time with God." But doing so while things fall apart around us can be a clear indication of our true relationship with God.

On November 22, 1873, the passenger ship SS Villa De Havre was accidentally rammed and sunk by another ship, the Lockhern. Four little girls were among those who drowned. The surviving mother sent word to her husband, Horatio Gates Spafford, to join her and mourn the deaths of their daughters. Mr. Spafford set sail in December to cross the Atlantic. At one point in the crossing, the captain quietly informed Mr. Spafford that they would soon pass over the open-sea graves of his little girls. For most of us, a tragedy like this might lead to bitterness and cause us to turn away from God. But on that grief-filled night Horatio Spafford penned moving words of peace despite his heart full of pain. He wrote:

When peace like a river attendeth my way,
When sorrows like sea-billows roll:
Whatever my lot, Thou hast taught me to say,
It is well, it is well, with my soul.

We can be at peace with God in any situation because of the relationship we share and enjoy with him. Although our understanding of our trials and suffering may be unclear and their purpose forever unrevealed to us, we realize that such moments of anguish are a part of every life. All who live must suffer, and sometimes we must even suffer for God's purposes. Gratefully, God gives us hope and perseverance through the most difficult times. Paul's words in Romans 5:3-5 can describe us: "We also have joy with our troubles, because we know that these troubles produce patience. And patience produces character, and character produces hope. And this hope will never disappoint us, because God has poured out his love to fill our hearts. He gave us his love through the Holy Spirit, whom God has given us." In God's wisdom, he is at work through our calamities to develop something greater in us according to our faith and our desire to grow into his likeness. If we ask God for wisdom and discernment, he can teach us to use our most trying experiences for his glory and praise.

If we are determined to honor God in joy, sorrow, celebration and despair, then our thoughts will turn toward others for the purpose of revealing God to them as a source of comfort and love. This is a refreshing contrast to the world's ineffectual and demoralizing solutions to life's problems. In this kind of service, we will likely be drawn into a deeper, more meaningful walk with God. The seeds of inner peace can then begin to take root and grow within us.

In his book, *Come Before Winter and Share My Hope*, Dr. Charles Swindoll reminds us that "we become what we think about," and that our "thoughts, positive or negative, grow stronger when fertilized with constant repetition." Swindoll further explains that many people "who are cheery and enthusiastic continue to be so, even in the midst of difficult circumstances." On the other hand, when we think negative thoughts, we quite often allow ourselves to listen to all the lies Satan puts into our minds. Thus he degrades our walk with God, and we may find ourselves becoming stagnant and unproductive in the Lord's work.

Maintaining positive control of our attitude toward the Holy Spirit is essential if we intend to keep Satan from choking out all hope of finding inner peace. Paul warns us in Galatians 5:19-21, "The wrong things the sinful self does are clear: Being sexually unfaithful, not being pure, taking part in sexual sins, worshiping gods, doing witchcraft, hating, making trouble, being jealous, being angry, being selfish, making people angry with each other, causing divisions among people, feeling envy, being drunk, having wild and wasteful parties, and doing other things like these. I warn you now as I warned you before: Those who do these things will not inherit God's kingdom." The Lord Jesus issued a frightening warning to those who do not keep their minds filled with thoughts that are wholesome and fertile ground for the Spirit's workings: "When an evil spirit comes out of a person, it travels through dry places, looking for a place to rest. But when it finds no place, it says, 'I will go back to the house I left.' And when it comes back, it finds that house swept clean and made neat. Then the evil spirit goes out and brings seven others spirits more evil than it is, and they go in and live there. So the person has even more trouble than before" (Luke 11:24-26). What are you allowing to fill your mind and heart?

Attitudes that work against the holiness of the Spirit are not pleasing to God and only work to destroy our peace of mind. Perhaps we may even cause a brother or sister to stumble because of our critical, unforgiving, sinful natures. Many of us find it easier to hold grudges and refuse to forgive those who have wronged us than to offer them the same grace God gave. To our shame, as Rubel Shelly puts it, "We don't forgive them – we parole them." And our failure to forgive others taints our own souls.

Jesus sharply rebuked Peter for denying that his Master would suffer and be killed. "Go away from me, Satan!" He castigated the misguided apostle. "You are not helping me! You don't care about the things of God, but only about the things people think are important" (Matthew 16:23). Jesus' purpose in coming to earth was to die for mankind. Peter tempted Christ to seek life, not death, and therefore his protest was a stumbling block to Jesus. How often do we find our own wrong attitudes and mistaken values causing us to seek something besides "the things of God?" In such moments we are headed away from the peace that comes only from him.

Paul instructed the Christians in Rome to "stop judging each other." He told them, "We must make up our minds not to do anything that will make another Christian sin. So let us try to do what makes peace and helps one another" (Romans 14:13, 19). "Our sinful selves want what is against the Spirit," he cautioned his converts elsewhere (Galatians 5:17). But if we allow the Spirit to nurture our souls, he will fill us with all manner of good things. "The Spirit produces the fruit of love, joy, peace, patience, kindness, goodness, faithfulness, gentleness, self-control" (Galatians 5:22-23).

So the Scriptures show that what we allow to enter our minds is critical to our relationship with God and to any hope we may have of finding inner peace. If we let God's

Spirit shape our thoughts and attitudes, we reap a double blessing, for he both calms our own souls and, simultaneously, spurs us on to do good for others. Have you noticed how often the Scriptures link what is going on inside our hearts with what we are doing for the Lord?

1. "Be joyful because you have hope. Be patient when trouble comes, and pray always. Share with God's people who need help. Bring strangers in need into your homes" (Romans 12:12-13).

2. "Brothers and sisters, think about the things that are good and worthy of praise. Think about the things that are true and honorable and right and pure and beautiful and respected. Do what you learned and received from me, what I told you, and what you saw me do. And the God who gives peace will be with you" (Philippians 4:8-9).

3. "If a person's thinking is controlled by the sinful self, there is death. But if their thinking is controlled by the Spirit, there is life and peace" (Romans 8:6).

Contentment and peace can be found while we actively pray with humility for the Holy Spirit to show us our sinful attitudes. Thus we can begin to make the necessary changes in our lives by replacing our negative thinking with thoughts that are pleasing to God. In this process, God brings nourishment and refreshment to our souls. "You were taught to be made new in your hearts, to become a new person," Paul reminded his converts (Ephesians 4:23-24). Peace is one blessing we gain through such renewal. "You, Lord, give true peace to those who depend on you, because they trust you," the prophet acknowledged as he praised God (Isaiah 26:3). God gives us peace for the same reason.

For the most part, we are in control of what enters our mind. We control what we allow to remain there. God helps wholesome thinking by providing guidelines for us to follow and to store in our hearts for seasons of refreshment. Inner peace is thus promoted by our dependence and trust in God to work in us what is pleasing to him.

Many passages in the Bible deal with faith and trust in

God. We can constructively use these Scriptures to change our thought patterns to develop inner peace. Notice that while we learn to trust in the Almighty, we also take an active part in the process.

1. "I leave you peace; my peace I give you. I do not give it to you as the world does. So don't let your hearts be troubled or afraid" (John 14:27).

2. "Let the peace that Christ gives control you thinking, because you were all called together in one body to have peace. Always be thankful" (Colossians 3:15).

3. "Do not worry about anything, but pray and ask God for everything you need, always giving thanks. And God's peace, which is so great we cannot understand it, will keep your hearts and minds in Christ Jesus" (Philippians 4:6-7).

Daily reciting of scriptures that encourage development of inner peace takes diligence and prayer. But the endeavor yields its rewards if we are actively striving to replace negative thoughts with positive images. In 1 Peter 3:10-12 the apostle promises, "A person must do these things to enjoy life and have many happy days. He must not say evil things, and he must not tell lies. He must stop doing evil and do good. He must look for peace and work for it. The Lord sees the good people and listens to their prayers."

When we face suffering and adversity, it is normal for our human nature to become hurt, angry, or disillusioned. Many of us can see our own questions reflected in Habakkuk's passionate cry: "Lord, how long must I ask for help and you ignore me? I cry out to you about violence, but you do not save us! Why do you make me see wrong things and make me look at trouble? People are destroying things and hurting others in front of me; they are arguing and fighting. So the teachings are weak, and justice never comes. Evil people gain while good people lose. The judges no longer make fair decisions." Then the Lord speaks these amazing words to his prophet, "Look at the nations! Watch them and be amazed and shocked. I will do something in your lifetime that you won't believe even when you are told about it'" (Habakkuk 1:1-5). It will strengthen us to remember that God provides his Holy Spirit to nurture and promote our peace with him at these times. A consistent trusting relationship with God is crucial to our well-being. It gives us the comfort and support we want and need.

As an example of this, let us look to Christ, who throughout his ministry taught and comforted his followers with words describing the peace that comes from above to all who will put their faith and trust in him (Matthew 21:21-22). His words carry added impact when we consider that he knew the type of death that awaited him. Despite the cross that loomed before our Lord, he carried with him the peace that can only come from an abiding trust in God.

Jesus suffered much to fulfill God's plan of salvation for us. He not only endured physical torture on the cross, but he also suffered mental and emotional anguish. He was separated from his Father at the time when he needed God's comfort and presence most. On the cross he cried out, "My God, my God, why have you rejected me?" (Matthew 27:46). Some suggest that it is against God's nature to associate with sin, so he had to separate himself from his Son, thus provoking that impassioned cry from Jesus when he took our sins upon himself. "Christ had no sin, but God made him become sin so that in Christ we could become right with God" (2 Corinthians 5:21). "Surely the Lord's power is enough to save you," Isaiah told his people. "He can hear you when you ask for help. It is your evil that has separated you from your God. Your sins cause him to turn away from you, so he does not hear you" (59:1-2). When we suffer, we often feel separated from God just as Jesus did.

In Romans 5:20-21, Paul writes, "The law came to make sin worse. But when sin grew worse, God's grace increased. Sin once used death to rule us, but God gave people more of his grace so that grace could rule by making people right with him. And this brings life forever though Jesus Christ our Lord." Through Christ's act of obedience to death, sinners are redeemed to God by his shed blood. From the Son come all the blessings (including inner peace) for those who wear his name.

Jesus did not relish the agony of the cross, but he wanted to do the will of his Father. This is poignantly seen in his prayer in Gethsemane. " 'Father, if you are willing, take away this cup of suffering. But do what you want, not what I want.' Then an angel from heaven appeared to him to strengthen him" (Luke 22:42-43). With Christ's obedience to his Father's will, he gained strength and comfort, and surely peace. In our obedience to God, we can also know the peace that comes by putting our trust in him.

In this book I have recounted for you some dark days of my life, not to seek your pity but to validate my message. It is precisely because of the tragedies and trials I've struggled through that I can tell you with assuredness that inner peace is possible, although achieving it does not mean that we won't experience grief and anguish. We will definitely feel these emotions and suffer pain. We cannot escape them while living in an imperfect, sinful world, but we can draw from an over-riding Power within us. God's Holy Spirit will sustain us with God's peace during times of struggle and heartache if we truly want to seek him and to remain faithful to him.

From what I've told you, you know that I haven't always had inner peace. I know from hard experience that it takes constant discipline and prayer to maintain it. There are moments still when I wrestle with the question of whom I will listen to – God or Satan.

I hope that sharing my personal experiences has helped you to see how that each bludgeoning of my soul has served as a later stepping stone in my journey to inner peace. I believe God used these problems to bring me to a clearer understanding of the peace he wants me to have in my heart.

In Mrs. Charles E. Cowan's Streams in the Desert, I like the way she describes how God brings about his solutions as we weather the storms of life:

Some storms of life come suddenly: a great sorrow, a bitter disappointment, a crushing defeat. Some come slowly. They appear upon the ragged edges of the horizon no larger than a man's hand, but, trouble that seems so insignificant spreads until it covers the sky and overwhelms us.

Yet it is in the storm that God equips us for service. When God wants an oak, he plants it on the moor where the storms will shake it and the rains will beat down upon it. It is in the midnight battle with elements that the oak wins its rugged fiber and becomes the king of the forest.

When God wants to make a man, he puts him into some storm. The history of manhood is always rough and rugged. No man is made until he has been out into the surge of the storm. No one is complete without the sublime fulfillment of the prayer, "O God, make me, break me, and make me."

The beauties of nature come after the storm. The rugged beauty of the mountain is born in a storm, and the heroes of life are the storm-swept and the battle-scarred.

Perhaps one day I can exclaim with Paul, "For this reason I am happy when I have weaknesses, insults, difficulties, sufferings, and all kinds of troubles for Christ. Because when I am weak, then I am truly strong" (2 Corinthians 12:10). And, "In all these things we have full victory through God who showed his love for us" (Romans 8:37). I am still learning the process and have not yet mastered "delighting" in adversity. Nevertheless, God continues to bless me with new stages of inner peace, for which I am grateful each day.

Conclusion

God continually works on my attitude and brings my focus back into his Spirit-filled perspective on perseverance, acceptance, and grace. He leads me repeatedly to seek his counsel and guidance through earnest prayer. Here are some suggestions that may help you find inner peace in your life:

- Pray constantly that God will give you peace (Psalm 122:6; 1 Timothy 5:5).
- Pray for the Holy Spirit to reveal to you your sinful nature and to help you overcome it (Ephesians 1:17-18).
- Daily strive to have wholesome and positive thoughts (2 Peter 3:1).
- Develop an attitude of faith and trust in God (Matthew 21:21-22; John 14:1).
- Pray for God's direction and guidance (Proverbs 1:5).
- Trust God to enable and empower your efforts (Proverbs 3:5-6; Luke 1:74; Acts 4:29-30; Acts 14:3).
- Develop an abiding relationship with God (Ephesians 3:16-21).
- Recognize God as Lord and Master of your life (Psalm 16:2, 7; Psalm 20:5; 2 Timothy 2:21).
- Guard against harboring negative thoughts and atti tudes (Jeremiah 4:14; Genesis 6:5).

- Think about and recite passages from the Bible daily; sing and listen to songs of praise to God (Deuteronomy 31:30; 32:45-47).
- Allow God's Holy Spirit to give you comfort, joy, and peace, especially during times of trial and hardship (1 Thessalonians 1:6; 2 Corinthians 1:3-4; Romans 14:17).
- Practice being kind to others even when you don't want to or when you think they don't deserve it (The Golden Rule – Luke 6:31-35).
- Recognize the hand of God in your blessings and immediately give him your humble thanks, praise, and glory (Psalm 13:6; Psalm 22:23, 26).
- Visualize peaceful thoughts (1 Peter 3:11).
- Always remember that forgiveness plays a part in the inner peace process (Luke 11:4; 2 Corinthians 2:7).
- In spite of all the stress and the trials Satan hurls your way, never forget that God loves you and cares for you (Zephaniah 2:7; 3:17; Exodus 34:6; Deuteronomy 7:13; Psalm 23).

This poem, A Purpose in Pain, was entered in a Poetry contest on healing and took an award. My very dear friend, Claire Ross, wrote it especially for me. It was such a humbling, yet delightful surprise. Because she so honored me with these kind words, I am pleased to share them with you. May they encourage you on your quest for inner peace, is my prayer.

A Purpose In Pain

Her life from the very beginning
Brought tragedy, hard to transcend,
But a spirit of gentleness filled her
And helped her survive and to mend.
As a child, a friend of the family
Molested her, filled her with fear.
In High School her brother was murdered,
The reasons were never made clear.
In later years MS attacked her,
Robbed her of health in her prime.
She accepted it bravely and calmly,
Taking only one step at a time.
Her trust in the Lord kept her going
As she pondered the meaning of life –
She wondered why some had to suffer,
Cope with anguish and terrible strife.
One day she decided her story
Was one other people should know.
She would share in a book all her heartache,
How adversity helped her to grow.
She'd learned perseverance and patience,
Believing each day was a step
Leading on to a Heavenly Kingdom
Where all of the tears she had wept
Would be washed away in an instant
And the glory of God she would see,
She would run and never be tired –
She would fly, and like eagles be free.
Day and night she wrote down her story,
Every detail, with joy, was expressed.
Inner peace filled her heart as she penned it –
With each line she was quietly blessed.
Her book gave a purpose for living,
As she shared all her suffering and pain,
Helping others endure brought healing,
And proved her life wasn't in vain.

– Claire Ottenstein Ross

Bibliography

Anderson, Ann Kiemel. *Women's Devotional Bible Calendar.* Grand Rapids: Zondervan, 1993.

Aristotle. *Friendship Calendar.* Marshalltown: Thoughtful Books, 1989.

Aristotle. *Secret Pal. Chatham* Publications, 1994.

Clarendon, Edward. *Friendship Calendar.* Marshalltown: Thoughtful Books, 1989.

Cowan, Mrs. Charles E. *Streams in the Desert.* Grand Rapids: Zondervan, 1965.

Fox, Tami. *A 3rd Serving of Chicken Soup for the Soul.* Deerfield Beach, Health Communications, 1996.

Graham, Ruth Bell. *Women's Devotional Bible Calendar.* Grand Rapids: Zondervan, 1993.

Grant, Amy. *"All I Ever Have To Be."* 1980.

Haverman, E. *For Couples in Love Calendar.* Bloomington: Garborg's, 1995.

Keller, Helen. *2nd Helping, Chicken Soup for the Soul.* Deerfield Beech, Health Communications, 1996.

Kempis, Thomas A. *For Couples in Love Calendar.* Bloomington: Garborg's, 1995.

Kuykendall, Carol. *Women's Devotional Bible Calendar.* Grand Rapids: Zondervan, 1993.

Lucado, Max. *God's Inspirational Promise Book.* Dallas: Word, 1996.

Lucado, Max. *He Still Moves Stones.* Dallas: Word, 1993.

Narramore, Kathy and Alice Hill. Women's Devotional Bible Calendar. Grand Rapids: Zondervan, 1993.

Osbeck, Kenneth W. *Hymn Stories*. Grand Rapids: Kregel, 1982.

Paula. *"Friend"*, 1990. (A quote from stationery.)

Peale, Norman Vincent. *The Power of Positive Thinking*. Grand Rapids: Zondervan, 1988.

Peter, Lawrence J. *Peter's Quotations*. New York: Quill, 1977.

Rikkers, Doris. *Women's Devotional Bible Calendar*. Grand Rapids: Zondervan, 1993.

Shelly, Rubel. *"We Don't Forgive Them . . ."* Lecture at Freed-Hardeman College, 1976.

Smith, Hannah Whithall. *Women's Devotional Bible Calendar*. Grand Rapids: Zondervan, 1993.

Swindoll, Charles. *Come Before Winter and Share My Hope*. Grand Rapids: Zondervan, 1985.

Webster, Daniel. *Webster's Standard Dictionary*. Cleveland: MacMillan, 1986.

Yancey, Philip. *Disappointment With God*. Grand Rapids: Zondervan, 1988.